The Forest Feast
ROAD TRIP

Simple Vegetarian Recipes Inspired by My Travels Through California

written, photographed,
and illustrated by

erin gleeson

Abrams,
New York

The Santa Cruz Mountains

CALIFORNIA
1

Humboldt

Lassen

Tahoe

Mendocino

Sacramento

Sonoma/Napa

Yosemite

San Francisco

Monterey

Eastern Sierras

Big Sur

Santa Barbara

Los Angeles

Palm Springs/
Joshua Tree

San Diego

for Winnie ♡

the best (and only)
reason I can think of
to buy a minivan

Half Moon Bay

Big Sur

Campovida winery, Hopland (here & right)

California poppies blooming in the spring at Russian Ridge Preserve in the Santa Cruz Mountains near where we live

Contents

10 Homes on the Road

⑥

During our year of road trips, we stayed in ten cabins, cottages, beach houses, and other unique homes around California. Follow the page numbers below to see photos of each destination.

⑧

⑦

⑨

⑩

⑥ a small cabin on a lavender farm in the Eastern Sierras, page 132

⑦ a ranch house on the bay near Humboldt, page 156

⑧ a desert home we rented near Palm Springs, page 204

⑨ a rustic mid-century home overlooking the ocean at the Sea Ranch, page 224

⑩ an octagonal house we rented in Tahoe, page 230

Santa Barbara

Introduction

I grew up in California, and I thought I knew her pretty well. Los Angeles, San Francisco, Yosemite! Avocados, oranges, Cabernet! So, returning to California ten years ago after several years in New York felt like coming home. I grew up in Sonoma County, but when we left Brooklyn, Jon and I moved a few hours south of there, to the Santa Cruz Mountains. We found a little cabin in the woods that inspired me to create vegetarian cookbooks with our new abundance of year-round produce using my own photography and watercolor illustrations.

Most of our trips were back to the East Coast to see family and friends, or farther afield like our extended trip to Europe that inspired my last cookbook, *The Forest Feast Mediterranean*. I'd almost taken for granted that I lived in this Golden State, but knew I wanted to explore parts of it I had never been to or hadn't experienced since I was little. So, in search of adventure and culinary inspiration, we piled our family into our Nissan Pathfinder, downloaded a bunch of podcasts, and set off exploring California from the Mexico border to the massive sequoias of Humboldt County. We did one long trip—2,500 miles without leaving the state—and several small side trips to explore different regions. Since we started off on our first trip, two big additions have entered our lives: our third child, Winnie, and subsequently, a minivan we call Carlene.

Cooking in our cabin surrounded by nature has brought me so much creative inspiration, and I wanted to take that idea on the road. Between chapters you will find photos of the ten different places we stayed around California—cabins, cottages, beach houses, and other unique dwellings—and fun things we discovered near each. We found most of the accommodations on vacation rental sites; we were looking for places that were affordably unique and not too extravagant. We stayed in a yurt on an urban farm in downtown Los Angeles, a cabin near Big Sur with an outdoor bathtub, and a lofted octagonal house in Lake Tahoe. We saw elephant seals in Cambria and summer snow in Lassen Volcanic National Park. We hit the slopes in the Sierras and went rafting on the Truckee River. And explored more farmers' markets than you can imagine!

Although California is a melting pot of cultures now, as we drove, we were reminded of the complex and troubling stories, both past and present, that make up the story of this state. It's essential to remember the rich culture of the Native American people who have been living in California for centuries. We passed towns and state parks named for Native Americans. One of the most powerful places we visited was the Paiute Cultural Center in the Eastern Sierras where we learned about how the Paiute gathered and grew food. Today they are committed to growing unique varieties of plants and vegetables that connect to the area's first inhabitants.

A must-stop location in the Eastern Sierras is Manzanar, a museum on the site of a former Japanese internment camp from WWII, which details the devastating account of how the United States imprisoned our own citizens because of widespread xenophobia. Furthermore, in the Central Valley and throughout California we know it's often migrant farm workers who pick the strawberries, grapes, and lettuce that feed much of America. It's essential that we continue to strive for good working conditions and strong labor laws while we enjoy the literal fruits of all their hard labor. Healthy and tasty food needs also to be picked ethically!

California is diverse not only culturally and geographically but agriculturally, and our goal was to explore what's grown along the way. We visited farms, ranches, orchards, wineries, and more. We saw papayas for sale at farmers' markets in the south, bright leafy kale in the foggy markets of the north, and endless rows of almond trees in the Central Valley. We met date farmers in the Mojave Desert, watched brussels sprouts being harvested by the beach, and picked oranges for breakfast in Palm Springs. We tasted grapes in Sonoma, hiked through wildflowers in the Santa Cruz Mountains, and surfed in Santa Barbara. Throughout it all, we picked, cooked, and ordered some incredible food.

Culinary inspiration on the road helped me create these recipes. We stayed on a lavender farm in the Sierras that prompted the shortbread on page 214, and the apricots we picked on the Central Coast led to the salsa on page 138. California has amazing Mexican food, so you'll see lots of that in these pages, too. Some of these recipes are great for a road trip or picnic, others are perfect for cooking at home.

After more than a year of road trips to create this book, we still love being on the road, meeting new people, trying new food, and exploring nooks and crannies we'd never heard about. Simply put, California is spectacular and road tripping is a great way to see it. Although we shot much of this book before the COVID-19 pandemic hit, we continued road tripping around California. Suddenly driving felt like the only safe way to travel, and we set off in our minivan to explore some more. We loved road trips before, but I think the realities of life after COVID have made us much more apt to continue traveling this way in the future.

This is not a guidebook, but rather a cookbook that's an homage to California and to being on the road. California is huge and there are still so many places I haven't been. Death Valley, the Yuba River, and Ojai are on my list. But in these pages, you'll find photos and stories of places we stumbled upon that weren't on my list, and that's what makes road trips so much fun.

I don't love driving in my daily life, but there's something different about setting out on the open road. Once you settle into a long drive, the thoughts of everyday life turn to white noise and your mind becomes serene. The kids fall asleep, you get into the music, the scenery is amazing, and you're in the groove. Add some good car snacks, a well-planned hike stop, and a spectacular new destination and you've got yourself a road trip. Sure, there are bumps in the road, flat tires, terrible Google map rerouting, hangry kids, and spilled snacks, but versions of that happen at home, too, so why not explore a new place while you're at it.

While this book is California-centric, my hope is that it'll spark wanderlust wherever you live. You don't need to be in California to find most of the ingredients I use, and the recipes remain simple, approachable, vegetarian fare to share with friends and family. No matter where in the world you are or how well you think you know it, I hope you'll take a drive and look for something new. You never know what inspiration you'll find to bring home.

Happy cooking!

Erin

For trip resources and more photos visit theforestfeast.com and follow along @theforestfeast. Tag recipes you make from this book #ForestFeastRoadTrip

the
Santa
Cruz
Mountains

Over the course of about a year we
took many road trips around California,
starting from our home in the Santa
Cruz Mountains (here & right).

At home in the Santa Cruz
Mountains (here & left)

De La Cour Ranch,
Lone Pine (here & right)

tips for using this book

This cookbook features recipes inspired by farms we visited, ingredients we saw growing, friends we cooked with, and restaurants we ate at while traveling around California. Some have become weeknight staples in our home, some are great for entertaining, and some are perfect for packing on a road trip or picnic.

RECIPES serve 4-6
unless otherwise noted

MEASUREMENTS

T	tablespoon
t	teaspoon
C	cup
kg	kilogram
g	gram
cm	centimeter
mm	millimeter
in	inch
L	liter
ml	milliliter

a few of my kitchen staples
(that you might not have on hand):

Bragg Liquid Aminos: I use this instead of soy sauce and I love the flavor.

Tajín: This powdered Mexican seasoning is salty, limey, a bit spicy, and great on fresh fruit and cucumbers.

Old Bay: I put this salty, slightly spicy seasoning mix on everything from roasted vegetables to avocado toast to hard-boiled eggs.

Meyer lemons: These are prevalent in California and are thought to be a cross between a lemon and an orange, making them a bit sweeter. You can always use a regular lemon if you can't find them.

when sautéing, I use medium heat unless otherwise noted

SALT { I use coarse or kosher salt when cooking & flaky Maldon sea salt to serve.

Big
Sur

On our way down Hwy 1, we stopped in
Big Sur for a few nights and stayed
at this idyllic cabin. It was secluded
and peaceful with a stunning view.

The big kitchen window & deck look out on a canyon of trees.

Antiques filled the bedroom, which felt like a treehouse.

I loved the indoor/outdoor flow of kitchen to deck.

Beside the cabin is a wood-fired sauna.

Breakfast at the cabin before heading out for the day

We stopped for a snack at the famous Big Sur Bakery.

View from Hwy 1 driving south

Wildflower & cactus-filled hike

A soak in the outdoor
tub at the cabin after
a day of exploring

There's nothing I love more than a meal with a view, and this one might top them all. Big Sur's famous restaurant Nepenthe is a must-stop, and I loved their California Beet Salad. Be sure to visit their well-curated gift shop on your way out.

When driving down Hwy 1 we stopped at
McWay Falls, where there's an easy path
to see this iconic Big Sur vista. It's
part of Julia Pfeiffer Burns State Park.

Pfeiffer Beach (here & right), part of Los Padres National Forest in Big Sur, is one of the most majestic beaches I have ever visited.

SNACKS

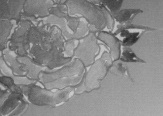

California Grazing Board

serves 4-6

Driving through the rolling green coastal hills near Tomales (below) we could see why the area was known for its cheese! Grab your biggest cutting board to create this colorful cheese platter. My board at right is 16 x 20 in (40 x 50 cm). You can also cover a baking tray with parchment or put butcher paper directly on your table and start building. By piling it all together instead of separating items into bowls it creates a pretty collage, plus the cleanup is easier! I like to choose local cheeses whenever possible, like this Point Reyes blue, which comes from the cape near Tomales Bay. My ideas here are just suggestions—feel free to use in-season produce and have fun with it. You can even let color guide you; I chose a warm color palette here, selecting items that were mostly red, orange, yellow, and pink.

You'll need:

cheese: about 3 oz (85 g) per person. I chose 3 different hardnesses and shapes: one creamy round, one blue wedge, and one hard cheese broken into rough bits (instead of cut). I looked for cheeses local to my area.

crackers: I buy 2 types with differing flavors and shapes.

olives

cherry tomatoes

radishes with the stem on

raspberries

clementines

orange: I sliced a Cara Cara orange into half-wheels (peel on).

nuts: Marcona almonds & roasted cashews

dried fruit: peaches & pears

build your board:

Begin by placing the cheese and larger items in separate areas of the board. Next add crackers in 3 or 4 spots, fanning them out in curved lines. Next add a snaky row of orange slices. Arrange medium items, like the radishes, in groups of 3. Continue placing the ingredients in little piles to cover the entire board. When it's mostly full, decorate with fresh sprigs of herbs, like rosemary, edible flowers, and any other garden clippings or unique fruits (like the golden berries I found here).

View from Elephant Rocks near Tomales

Beet Hummus
WITH PARSNIP FRIES
serves 4-6

While in Santa Barbara, we had a beach picnic and brought beet hummus we found at the Isla Vista Food Co-op. We ate it with slices of a cucumber that we picked the day before at Rancho San Julian (page 52). At home, I played around with the recipe and found it delicious with parsnip fries. When putting the hummus in a bowl, I use a spoon to create a little well on the top and drizzle with olive oil before serving.

for the hummus

1 (15 oz/430 g) can chickpeas, drained
½ small raw beet
½ c (120 ml) olive oil
¼ c (60 g) tahini paste
1 clove garlic
juice from ½ lemon
salt & pepper

Blend all ingredients in a food processor or blender until smooth

Add a bit more oil if needed, to achieve desired consistency.

for the fries

Trim & slice 8 large parsnips lengthwise into about 6 strips. Lay out on a baking sheet and drizzle generously with olive oil and sprinkle with Old Bay seasoning.

Bake at 425°F (220°C) for 20-25 min (toss once) or until golden & tender

Devereux Beach in Isla Vista

Spring Ricotta Platter

Our friend Debbie runs a farm in Los Altos Hills, and we stopped by in the spring to pick snap peas and oranges. I came home and made this snacking platter, which works well as an appetizer or alongside soup for lunch.

(1) 1 large handful snap peas,
    trimmed & sliced
5 radishes, cut into matchsticks
3 sprigs mint, chopped
2 T pepitas
1 T olive oil
squeeze of clementine juice
salt & pepper

} *toss in a bowl*

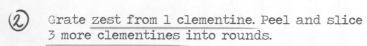

(2) Grate zest from 1 clementine. Peel and slice
3 more clementines into rounds.

(3) Spread 6 oz (170 g) ricotta out on a platter or large plate.

(4) Fan out slices from the clementines over the ricotta.

(5) Pile the pea mixture in the middle and sprinkle the platter with salt, pepper, olive oil, and clementine zest.

serve with baguette slices & spoons for scooping the mixture onto the bread

Ezra & Max picking
snap peas with Debbie

Tahini Balls

makes about 25 balls

When traveling with kids, it's great to have healthy snacks on hand. These energy balls are just sweet enough that they'll eat them, but filling enough to keep them happy until the next meal. I also make these to send in their school lunches since they are nut-free. Somehow my kids always talk me into rolling them in sprinkles instead of sesame seeds, which is admittedly more fun.

1 c (145 g) dates
½ c (120 ml) tahini
1 c (85 g) oats
¼ c (60 ml) honey
} *blend in a food processor*

Pulse the mixture at first to get it well incorporated. It may be crumbly but it should stick together like a dough when pinched. Depending on the consistency of your tahini, you can add another spoonful of oats if the dough seems wet, or honey if it seems dry. The dough should be easy to roll into balls.

roll into approx. 1 T balls & roll each in sesame seeds

Max & Ezra snacking under a blooming nectarine tree on our friend's farm in Los Altos Hills

Blender Muffins
—3 WAYS—

makes 8-10 muffins

Our kids eat so much bread and pasta that I like to offer a flour-free snack sometimes. These come together quickly and are great for breakfast, for lunch with soup, or for a packed snack in the car. It's an adaptable recipe and I've made many variations, throwing in bits of different vegetables, and the kids still eat them. I got the idea to make them in a blender from my friends Sonja and Alex Overhiser, cookbook authors behind the website A Couple Cooks; these recipes are inspired by their Healthy Banana Bread Muffins. I often top them with a sprinkling of oats, but you can get creative by stirring nuts or dried berries into the batter or putting them on top of the muffins before baking.

Combine all ingredients in a blender, adding the oats last.
Blend until smooth then pour into greased muffin tins.

BASE RECIPE

2 bananas
2 eggs
¼ c (60 ml) olive oil
¼ c (60 ml) agave
or maple syrup
1 t baking powder
1 t baking soda
1 t cinnamon
pinch of salt
2 c (180 g) oats

GREEN MUFFINS

add 1 handful
fresh spinach

CARROT-RAISIN MUFFINS

add 1 medium carrot
(cut in chunks),
then after blending
stir in ½ c (75 g)
golden raisins

PUMPKIN MUFFINS

add ¾ c (180 ml)
pumpkin purée
from a can

Bake 25-30 min at 350°F (175°C)

A blanket of fog covers Silicon Valley below the Windy Hill Open Space Preserve trail in Woodside.

Root Vegetable Nachos

serves 4-6

California has amazing Mexican food, especially in the south near the border. This is my healthier take on nachos. You may wish to eat it with a fork.

1. 3 medium sweet potatoes, cut into wedges lengthwise, no need to peel
   5 parsnips, quartered lengthwise

lay out on a baking sheet, drizzle generously with olive oil, sprinkle with salt & bake at 425°F (220°C) for 20 min or until fork-tender with crispy edges

2-3 min before they come out of the oven, sprinkle with ⅔ c (75 g) grated white cheddar cheese (just long enough to melt)

2. Lay the cheesy, cooked vegetables on a platter & top with:

1 (15 oz/430 g) can black beans, drained & heated
3 scallions, chopped
⅔ c (165 ml) red salsa
½ c (75 g) black olives, sliced
1 (4 oz/113 g) can mild diced green chiles, drained
⅓ c (15 g) cilantro, chopped
½ c (120 ml) sour cream

These can be made vegan by skipping the cheese and using a nondairy sour cream.

Joshua Tree National Park

Queso Fresco Garden Platter

serves 4-6

In Los Angeles, we stayed in a bohemian-inspired yurt on an urban farm (page 74).
On the way back one day, we stopped at a nearby Mexican market and picked up
a round of queso fresco, a mild Mexican fresh cheese that's great with a summer
BBQ meal. We had it as an appetizer with plantain chips (also from the market)
and fresh veggies while cooking a taco dinner in the outdoor kitchen.

6 oz (170g) queso fresco
5 oz (140g) plantain chips
1 cucumber, sliced in ovals
1 carrot, cut into sticks
8 radishes, halved

} arrange on a platter

Serve with a couple wedges of
lime, salt and Tajín seasoning
to sprinkle on the veggies and
cheese if you wish. Tajín is a
limey-spicy seasoning powder
that comes in a small bottle,
often in the produce section
of the market. This platter is
even better with a margarita
(see page 60).

Skyfarm Yurt, where we
stayed in Los Angeles

Mediterranean Nachos

serves 4-6

The majestic central coastline of California can at times feel Mediterranean! I love this appetizer because there is no cooking involved, making it easy to assemble on-site for a picnic.

7 oz (200 g) bag pita chips
¾ c (180 ml) hummus
½ c (120 ml) Greek yogurt
⅓ c (50 g) pitted kalamata olives, chopped
⅔ c (100 g) crumbled feta
1 tomato, diced
3 scallions, chopped
¼ c (13 g) chopped parsley
8 oz (225 g) canned chickpeas, drained
½ cucumber, cubed with skin on
¼ lemon
salt & pepper

On a platter, lay out all the pita chips. Next drop several dollops of hummus & Greek yogurt. Scatter all other ingredients over the platter and finish with a sprinkle of lemon juice, salt, and pepper.

Enjoy at room temperature.

View from the restaurant
Nepenthe in Big Sur

Pumpkin Deviled Eggs

serves 4-6

It's fun to travel to warm and sunny Palm Springs during the colder months. On Thanksgiving I always make deviled eggs as a happy hour snack while we cook. This year I added pumpkin to the filling and these were a hit!

6 hard-boiled eggs, peeled & halved,
  yolks removed

2 t spicy mustard
2 t mayonnaise
3 T pumpkin purée
salt & pepper
} mash with the yolks in a bowl

¼ c (40 g) pomegranate seeds
⅛ t paprika
} garnish

→ Spoon the yolk mixture into the egg white halves & garnish each with pomegranate seeds & papkrika

The house we rented in Palm Springs (page 204)

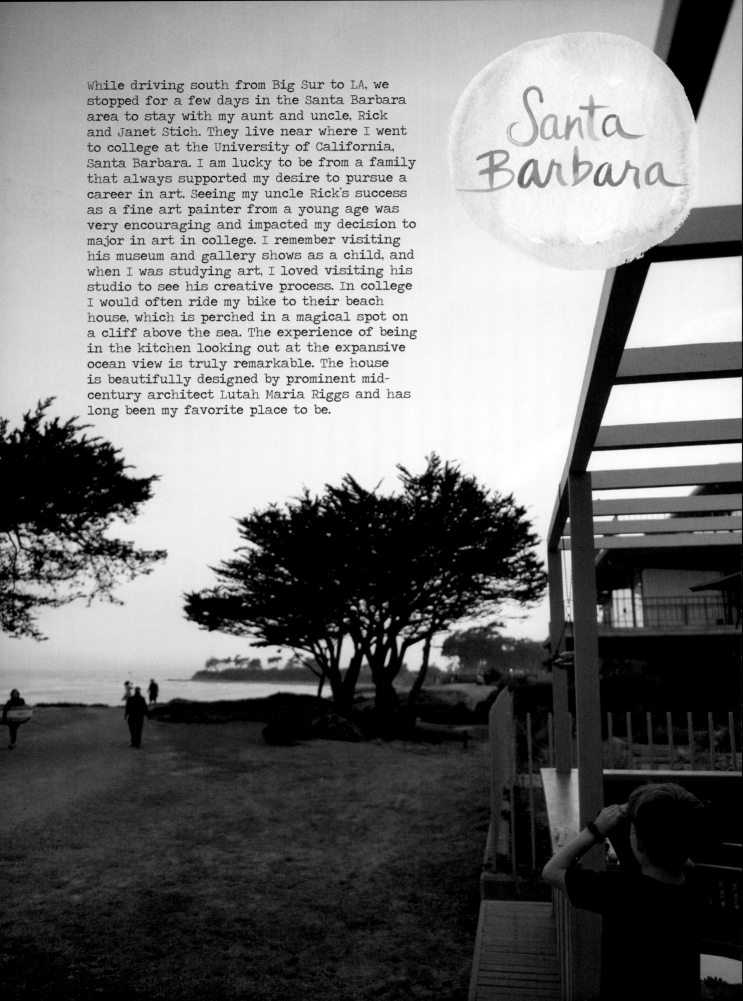

While driving south from Big Sur to LA, we
stopped for a few days in the Santa Barbara
area to stay with my aunt and uncle, Rick
and Janet Stich. They live near where I went
to college at the University of California,
Santa Barbara. I am lucky to be from a family
that always supported my desire to pursue a
career in art. Seeing my uncle Rick's success
as a fine art painter from a young age was
very encouraging and impacted my decision to
major in art in college. I remember visiting
his museum and gallery shows as a child, and
when I was studying art, I loved visiting his
studio to see his creative process. In college
I would often ride my bike to their beach
house, which is perched in a magical spot on
a cliff above the sea. The experience of being
in the kitchen looking out at the expansive
ocean view is truly remarkable. The house
is beautifully designed by prominent mid-
century architect Lutah Maria Riggs and has
long been my favorite place to be.

Santa
Barbara

My aunt and uncle's house near Santa Barbara

Here: the historic farmhouse at Fairview Gardens in Goleta, which has a farm stand and farm that is open to the public

MACARTHUR AVOCADOS $1 ea

Top right & bottom left: the Saturday morning farmers' market in downtown Santa Barbara

Here: a seaside picnic with my cousins at Shoreline Park in Santa Barbara

While in the Santa Barbara area in July, we stopped to visit my friend Elizabeth Poett at her family's ranch, Rancho San Julian. We picked apricots in the orchard and zucchini in the garden. In addition to selling ranch goods at the farmers' market, Elizabeth runs The Ranch Table, where she hosts classes, events, and dinners under the vine-covered dining area next to the historic farmhouse (see right).

Rancho
San Julian

Bottom
left: with
Elizabeth
Poett

Santa Barbara (here & right)

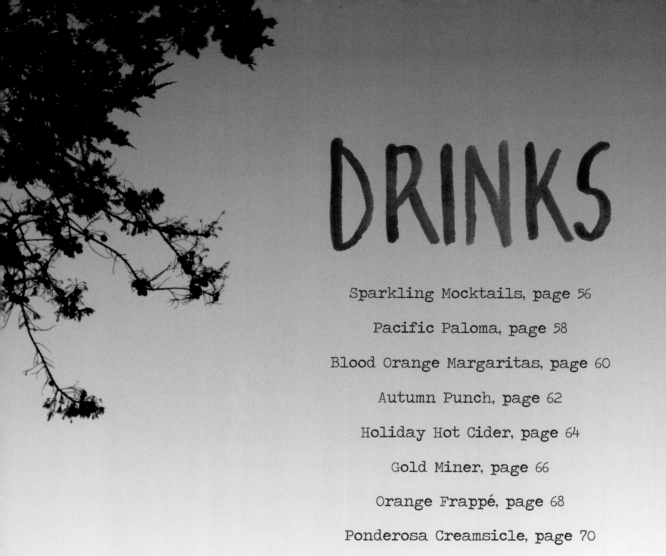

DRINKS

Sparkling Mocktails

recipes make 1 drink

I was pregnant with Winnie while making much of this book, and to keep happy hour fun I experimented with many nonalcoholic drinks. Here are some favorites that I'm still enjoying. They can also easily be spiked—add a shot of tequila to #1, add a shot of vodka to #2 and #4, and use regular beer for #3. Cheers!

① the Salty Watermelon

Pulse 1 c (150 g) cubed seedless watermelon and juice from 1 lime in a blender. Strain. Use the squeezed lime to wet the rim of a glass, dip the rim in coarse salt, add ice, then pour watermelon juice in. Top off with seltzer and carefully stir.

② Blackberry Fizz

In a glass with ice, pour 2 T blackberry-flavored store-bought shrub (a fruity drinking vinegar) and a few drops of bitters. Top the glass off with seltzer and stir. Garnish with a fresh blackberry and mint.

③ Meyer Lemon Shandy

Pour 4 oz (120 ml) cold lemonade into a glass, then fill the glass up with cold nonalcoholic beer. Garnish with a wedge of lemon.

④ Beet-Lemonade Spritzer

Pour equal parts lemonade and seltzer into a glass of ice. Add 1 thin, round slice of beet, stir to disperse the color, then remove. Garnish with a wheel of lemon.

Pacific Paloma

makes 1 drink

I love a cocktail on the ocean, and California makes that easy! We stopped for
a scenic drink on Hwy 1 near Big Sur at Rocky Point Restaurant.

stir in a mixing glass {
2 oz (60 ml) grapefruit juice
2 oz (60 ml) mezcal
2 oz (60 ml) seltzer
1 t agave

Salt the rim of a glass, put a wheel
of grapefruit in on one side, add
ice, then pour the juice mixture in.

BLOOD ORANGE
Margaritas

makes 1 drink

On a girls' weekend in winter to sunny San Diego, the weather was gorgeous and the farmers' market in Little Italy, where we stayed, was full of citrus. A highlight of the trip was a long afternoon spent eating tacos and sipping Blood Orange Margaritas. My friend Mara makes these every year and I have adapted her recipe here.

½ c (120 ml) blood orange juice from (about 2 oranges)
juice from ½ lime
2 oz (60 ml) silver tequila
1 oz (30 ml) Cointreau
ice
} shake

1 T coarse salt
1 T Tajín seasoning
} mix on a plate

(1) Rub a <u>blood orange half</u> around the edge of the glass then dip the rim in the salt & Tajín mixture.

(2) Add **ice** to the glass then pour the shaken tequila mixture into the glass. Garnish with a <u>wheel of blood orange</u>.

Autumn Punch

serves 6-8

This is a pretty way to serve a drink at a fall gathering. Use any mixing bowl and ladle and be creative with whatever in-season produce you can find, cutting things thinly to float on top. My suggestion below is a boozy punch, but you can easily fill the bowl with nonalcoholic sparkling cider or any mixture of seltzer and juice.

for the punch

1 (750 ml) bottle sparkling white wine (I use prosecco)
4 oz (120 ml) St. Germain elderflower liqueur
2 c (240 ml) white grape juice
10 shakes bitters
ice

→ *stir in a mixing bowl*

float on top

edible flowers (I used chamomile)
Fuyu persimmon, cut in rounds
lemon, cut in rounds
clementine, cut in rounds
apple, cut in rounds with core intact
figs, cut in rounds
star fruit, sliced
pomegranate seeds
fresh cranberries

Holiday Hot Cider

serves 6-8

This is festive for a holiday party or for cool-weather outdoor entertaining. It's inspired by the citrus orchards we saw all over Palm Springs. I usually make it in a slow cooker so that it can stay warm all evening and guests can help themselves. I leave out a bottle of rum for those who prefer it spiked.

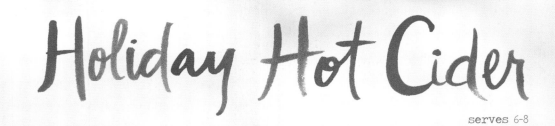

64 oz (2 L) unfiltered (cloudy) apple juice
juice from 5 clementines
5 cinnamon sticks

SIMMER ON LOW
stovetop: 30 min
slow cooker: 2-3 hours
(or until hot)

Just before serving, add round slices from 3 additional clementines and 1 c (95 g) fresh cranberries. Ladle into mugs and serve hot.

optional: add a shot of rum to individual glasses

Gold Miner

makes 1 drink

Bodie State Historic Park (below) was a fascinating stop in the Eastern Sierra region. We brought a picnic and explored this nineteenth-century gold-mining ghost town. Bodie feels frozen in time; peeking in the windows, you can see bottles still on the counter at the saloon and dishes on tables in homes (see page 136). My go-to cocktail at home is bourbon with a squeeze of clementine, and here I've added a bit of golden flare. The edible gold leaf flakes are completely optional, but relatively affordable online and especially fun if you're making these for guests.

2 oz (60 ml) bourbon
1 oz (30 ml) freshly squeezed orange or clementine juice
½ oz (15 ml) freshly squeezed lemon juice
1 t agave
ice

shake!

Pour into a glass with ice and garnish with a lemon twist and edible gold leaf flakes.

Bodie

Orange Frappé

serves 2

Put 2 peeled oranges and 10 ice cubes in a blender on high until the pulp has been very well incorporated and there are no chunks. (I use a Vitamix on high to get it as creamy and frothy as possible.)

Enjoy immediately before it separates.

Citrus growing at Flying Disc Ranch in Thermal

The famous Orange Julius drink was founded in California in the 1920s, and I remember my mother buying them for me as a treat when I was little. My version is very simple—just oranges—and is best made when they are sweet and in season.

Ponderosa Creamsicle

Each time my family visited Yosemite National Park when I was growing up, we always stopped after a day of hiking at the famous Ahwahnee Hotel for a drink and a treat from their historic sweet shop. It was fun to go back with Jon and the kids to continue this tradition. This time, since I was pregnant, I asked the bartender to recommend something nonalcoholic. This recipe is inspired by their famous Ponderosa Punch (named after the local pine tree), and it's a treat for adults and kids alike. It feels creamy but it's light, especially if you use a nondairy whipped cream.

ice
6 oz (180 ml) freshly squeezed clementine juice (or orange)
2 T coconut milk
seltzer
a few drops bitters
3 T whipped cream (I used a coconut-based nondairy whip)
1 slice clementine

Fill a tall glass halfway with ice. Then pour in the juice (it should come about halfway up the glass). Next add the coconut milk and bitters. Top the glass off with seltzer and gently stir. Garnish with a dollop of whipped cream and a slice of clementine. Serve with a spoon or straw.

Yosemite National Park

Rosé Spritz

serves 1

On warm summer evenings, we often do some gardening while the kids play. I love taking this refreshing and light drink outside with me. I plant edible flowers like nasturtium and snap dragons and often pop one in for a colorful garnish. You can often find edible flowers in the produce section of many grocery stores. This is also an easy drink to mix at a picnic.

rosé wine } EQUAL
seltzer   } PARTS
dash of bitters
ice

Stir and garnish with a lemon wheel and an edible flower.

Hwy 1 north of Santa Cruz

Skyfarm Yurt,
Los Angeles

In downtown Los Angeles, we stayed for a few nights at the amazing Skyfarm Yurt, a small urban farm thoughtfully created by husband-and-wife team Ilse Ackermann and Meeno Peluce. I fell in love with the outdoor kitchen and soaking tub, yurt bedroom, and plant-lined walkway to the shower. With the perennially moderate LA weather, this is outdoor living at its best.

One night at Skyfarm Yurt
we invited friends over for a
BBQ taco dinner on the deck.

Skyfarm Yurt,
Los Angeles

SALADS

Dressings

Lemons grow everywhere in California, and sometimes we have so many from friends' trees and our farm box that they end up in our salad dressings every day. When lemons run out, our go-to dressing is the sesame vinaigrette below. I love the flavor of the liquid aminos by Bragg (a California-based company!). It's similar to soy sauce but with a bit more umami.

① Everyday Sesame Vinaigrette

3 T Bragg Liquid Aminos (or soy sauce), ¼ c (60 ml) olive oil, ¼ c (60 ml) rice vinegar, 2 T sesame oil. Shake or whisk.

② Garlic Tahini Dressing

¼ c (60 ml) tahini, ¼ c (60 ml) olive oil, 3 T lemon juice (about 1 lemon), 2 t agave, 1 grated clove garlic, water to thin it out (add 1 t at a time to desired consistency). Whisk.

③ Meyer Lemon Vinaigrette

2 T minced shallots, zest from 1 Meyer lemon, 3 T Meyer lemon juice (about 1 lemon), ⅓ c (80 ml) olive oil, 2 t agave, 1 T white wine vinegar, salt & pepper. Whisk.

④ Creamy Avocado-Lime Dressing

½ avocado, ¼ c (60 ml) olive oil, 3 T lime juice (1-2 limes), ¼ c (10 g) cilantro (stems are OK!), 1 grated clove garlic, salt. Blend (I use a hand blender in a jar). Add water 1 t at a time to desired consistency.

BBQ Corn Salad

After a day of swimming in Lake Tahoe, we went back to the cabin
we rented (page 230) and made a simple BBQ dinner on the deck.
Food cooked outdoors always tastes better to me and the char-
ring of the corn adds so much flavor to this dish. If you
don't have a BBQ, try using a grill pan or broiling in the
oven on high until the kernels are slightly charred.

4 ears corn, husks removed
1 red bell pepper, diced
¼ red onion, finely diced
⅓ c (15 g) chopped cilantro
½ c (75 g) crumbled feta
juice from 1 lime
2 T olive oil
1 t Tajín seasoning (see page 42)

① BBQ the corn, turning occasionally,
for 3-5 min or until slightly charred.

② Cut the kernels off each cob and mix them
in a bowl with the other ingredients.

Lake Tahoe

Strawberry Caprese

serves 4-6

16 oz (455g) strawberries, trimmed & quartered
2 handfuls yellow cherry tomatoes, halved
1 handful basil leaves, torn into pieces
8 oz (225g) fresh mozzarella, torn into pieces

Scatter all ingredients on a platter and
drizzle with <u>olive oil</u>, <u>balsamic glaze
or vinegar</u>, and <u>flaky salt</u>.

In Pescadero we visited our friends
Kaeleigh and Airielle who run Fly Girl
Farm and helped pick strawberries for
them to take to the farmers' market.

Celery Slaw

serves 4-6

After visiting a date farm near Palm Springs (see page 206), I went home with more dates than I knew what to do with and began using them in sweet and savory dishes. This crunchy slaw is both tart and sweet and feels very fresh.

{ 8 celery stalks (about 1 small bunch),
  thinly sliced (I use a mandoline)
10 dates, pitted & chopped
½ c (50 g) sliced almonds
3 scallions, chopped

→ mix in a bowl

Dressing

whisk { 1 T grainy mustard
2 T olive oil
1 T rice vinegar
1 T maple syrup

↳ dress salad as desired, you may not wish to use it all

A date palm frond at Flying Disc Ranch in Thermal

Curry Cauliflower Salad

This salad is inspired by a dish cleverly called Cauli-fornia that we tasted at the inventive, vegetable-forward restaurant Satellite in down-town Santa Barbara. I love the contrasting sweetness of the grapes on top.

preheat oven to 425°F (220°C)

1 head cauliflower
olive oil
½ t garlic powder
½ t curry powder
salt & pepper
¾ c (115 g) sliced red grapes
⅓ c (40 g) sliced walnuts
2 scallions, chopped

1. Remove the florets from the head of cauliflower and spread out on a baking sheet. Sprinkle generously with olive oil, then with garlic powder, curry powder, and a few pinches of salt and pepper.

2. Bake at 425°F (220°C) for 30-35 min, or until the edges are golden, flipping once. Transfer to a platter and allow to cool.

3. Sprinkle the platter with the grapes, walnuts, and scallions, plus a bit of olive oil, salt and pepper to taste.

Picnic Salad

serves 2

I met my friend Jodie for a picnic and she packed her salad like this,
which I thought was so cute and useful since you can eat right out
of the jar. Put the heavier items on the bottom and pack it loosely so
it's easier to dress and toss.

- 1½ c (300 g) cooked lentils
- 8 mini potatoes, boiled & halved
- 1 carrot, grated
- ¼ red onion, diced
- 1 handful arugula

Divide the ingredients
between two 32-oz (960 ml)
wide-mouth jars, layering
the ingredients in the
order above. Bring a 4-oz
(120 ml) jar of your favorite
dressing (or one of mine,
see page 80) and pour some
in just before eating.
Shake, stir, and enjoy!

The elephant seals near Cambria are
quite a sight to see and definitely
worth a stop when driving down the
coast from Big Sur to Santa Barbara.

Palm Desert Salad

serves 4-6

The winter farmers' markets near Palm Springs are remarkable. In January we found dates, citrus, persimmons, and avocados! I came back to the house we rented (page 204) and made this salad for lunch.

4 handfuls mixed lettuce (look for red leaf & hearty winter lettuces)
1 c (30 g) loosely packed cilantro, chopped
2 Fuyu persimmons, cubed (peel on)
1 blood orange, peeled & sliced in rounds
juice from 1 blood orange
1 T olive oil
salt & pepper

Toss in a mixing bowl then add cubes from 1 <u>avocado</u> on top. Add a bit more oil if necessary to coat the greens.

The farmers' market in La Quinta

Coastal Quinoa Salad

serves 4-6

We spent a fun weekend in the town of Capitola, not far from Santa Cruz. We stayed near the river walk and could stroll to this beach that is adjacent to the downtown area. There are cute restaurants and shops, and the beach is perfect for kids.

{
- 2 c (370 g) cooked quinoa (about ¾ c/130 g dry quinoa cooked with 1⅓ c/315 ml water)
- ¾ c (110 g) raw corn kernels from a cob
- 15 cherry tomatoes, halved
- 1 c (65 g) chopped curly kale
- 1 c (95 g) thinly sliced purple cabbage
- ½ c (20 g) chopped cilantro
- ¼ c (35 g) roasted, salted sunflower seeds

toss in a bowl with olive oil, lime juice & salt

I love the colorful historic cottages on Capitola Beach, the Venetian Court Private Residences. A few are available as vacation rentals!

Foggy Beet & green Salad

Humboldt County, at the top of California, is known for its foggy weather, which makes for green grass and beautiful cheeses. Humboldt Fog, the iconic soft-ripened goat cheese famous for its bluish ribbon of edible ash, was created by Mary Keehn of Cypress Grove Dairy in Arcata, California. If you can't find this special cheese, try substituting a crumbled blue cheese or feta.

Slice 4 beets into ¼-inch (6-mm) rounds (no need to peel). Save the green tops if they had them. Lay the slices out on a baking sheet and drizzle generously with olive oil, salt, and pepper. Roast for 25 min at 400°F (205°C), or until fork-tender with a few crispy edges.

Spread 5 oz (140 g) baby arugula out on a platter. Drizzle with your favorite balsamic dressing. Lay the roasted beet slices in a row down the middle. Chop and quickly sauté the beet greens in a bit of butter until wilted (1-2 min) and place them over the beets.

Sprinkle the platter with small pieces of Humboldt Fog cheese (about 4 oz/115 g).

Trinidad

Kale & White Bean Salad

serves 4-6

In our weekly farm box subscription we get the most beautiful lacinato (or "dino" kale), which I love in this salad. If you can't find it, feel free to use any type of kale. Kale is so hearty that you can dress it lightly in the morning and pack it for lunch on the road, and it doesn't get soggy.

allow to marinate in a mixing bowl 5 min

1 (15 oz/430 g) can cannellini beans, drained & rinsed
1 T Bragg Liquid Aminos (see page 21)
1 T olive oil
1 T lemon juice

then mix in 2 small bunches <u>lacinato kale</u> (thinly sliced, stems removed) & ⅔ c (100 g) crumbled <u>feta</u>

Two days after leaving the heat of the desert, we were surprised (and the kids were thrilled!) to see snow on the ground in July in Lassen Volcanic National Park.

Sesame Potato Salad

serves 4-6

This is a hearty, filling salad to pack in a cooler or bring on a picnic. It's also an easy dish to prepare in a rental home if you bring along some cooked, canned lentils. I sometimes put this over a bed of salad greens to make it more of a meal.

24 oz (680 g) mini potatoes (about 16 potatoes)
½ red onion, diced
1½ c (300 g) cooked lentils
2 scallions, chopped
3 T chopped cilantro or basil

Halve and boil the mini potatoes for about 7 min or until fork-tender. Drain and transfer to a mixing bowl. Meanwhile, sauté the onion with a bit of <u>olive oil</u>, just until translucent (about 5 min), then add lentils and stir until everything is warm and combined (about 1 min). Add the lentil mixture to the potatoes and toss with some of the <u>Everyday Sesame Vinaigrette</u> on page 80. Serve warm or at room temperature, topped with scallions, herbs, <u>flaky salt, and pepper.</u>

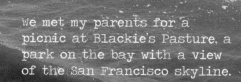

We met my parents for a picnic at Blackie's Pasture, a park on the bay with a view of the San Francisco skyline.

Lentil-Farro Salad

serves 4-6

It's nice to have some healthy, filling, and quick lunch options that aren't a sandwich while you're on the road, and this has become our go-to. I pack this salad into a big jar before leaving home, and it travels well in the cooler for a couple days. I bring a separate container of dressing to mix in before eating. Use your favorite vinaigrette or one of mine on page 80.

mix {
2 c (320 g) cooked farro
2 c (400 g) cooked lentils
4 mini cucumbers, sliced in thin rounds (peel on)
1 orange bell pepper, cubed
½ onion, diced
salt & pepper to taste

Redwood trees abut the beach in Humboldt County.

Sweet Potato & Black Bean Salad

serves 4-6

This colorful salad holds up well when packed for a picnic or served at a potluck.

2 sweet potatoes { cut into ½-in (1 cm) cubes (no need to peel) then sauté with 2 T <u>olive oil</u> & a bit of <u>salt</u> until fork-tender & slightly browned (10-15 min)

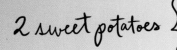

Cool potatoes in a mixing bowl & stir in:

1 (15 oz/430 g) can black beans, drained & rinsed
½ cucumber, cubed (no need to peel)
1 small red bell pepper, cubed
½ red onion, diced
handful cilantro, coarsely chopped

dressing

shake or whisk {
zest & juice from 2 limes
2 t honey or agave
1 T olive oil
salt
pinch of cayenne (optional)

Tomales Bay

Tomato Salad
with pistachio gremolata

serves 4-6

In Tahoe after a summer day of river rafting, we had a meal at the iconic
Sunnyside Lodge on the lake in Tahoe City, a restaurant my mom remembers
going to as a child with her family in the 1960s. I had a Caprese salad there
that inspired this recipe. Gremolata is like a chunky dressing or tapenade
to spread over the top of the tomatoes, and because the amount is small,
I find it easier to chop by hand than use a food processor.

for the gremolata:

¼ c (30 g) finely chopped roasted pistachios
¾ c (30 g) finely chopped cilantro
juice & zest from 1 lemon
1 clove garlic, grated
2 scallions, finely chopped
1 T olive oil
salt & pepper

→ MIX IN A BOWL

On a platter, lay out 5 in-season tomatoes cut into
round slices. Arrange 6 oz (170 g) burrata cheese
on top or on the side. Spoon the gremolata over
all, then sprinkle the platter with additional
olive oil, flaky salt, and pepper.

Rafting on the Truckee
River in Tahoe

Soba Salad

serves 4-6

We had so many great picnics by lakes in the eastern part of California. I especially loved June Lake. This salad is great when packed for lunch or a light dinner. I just keep the cilantro separate and add it right before eating.

① BOIL
{ 12 oz (400 g) soba noodles, boiled for about 4 min (see package)
{ strain & rinse under cold water
{ then transfer to a mixing bowl & add:

② WHISK → 1 T each {
olive oil
sesame oil
soy sauce
lime juice
sesame seeds
plus 1 clove garlic, grated

③ COMBINE → add to the bowl {
⅔ c (25 g) cilantro, coarsely chopped
⅔ c (105 g) shelled, cooked edamame
⅔ c (95 g) halved cherry tomatoes
8 oz (225 g) firm tofu, cut in strips & fried in olive oil, about 5 min per side

④ TOSS   all ingredients & enjoy at room temp

serve with lime wedges
& sriracha

June Lake

Big
Bear
Lake

We stayed in this charming A-frame near Big
Bear Lake for a few nights, and I loved the
light and the mid-century vibe. We enjoyed
days swimming and hiking nearby.

After breakfast at Grizzly Manor Cafe, we had to take a photo with one of the iconic wooden bears.

Downtown we found outdoor restaurants with live music.

We rented a boat on Big Bear Lake one afternoon.

We enjoyed hiking at Keller Peak, where we visited the fire tower and the Children's Forest.

SIDES

Big Bear Lake

Floral Flatbread

serves 4-6

During the early days of shelter-in-place, when everyone was home baking, the garden focaccia trend became quite popular. I first read about it in the *New York Times*. Inspired by a visit to the dahlia garden in August in Golden Gate Park, I decided to try something similar and took a shortcut by using store-bought pizza dough. This is all about being creative, so my ideas below are just suggestions. It would be fun to make these in a group with friends! I'd serve this with a glass of rosé from my favorite local winery, Thomas Fogarty.

16 oz (455g) pizza dough
olive oil
salt
red, orange, and/or
    yellow bell pepper
red onion
fresh flat-leaf parsley
fresh sage
fresh thyme
capers
pine nuts
dried basil or oregano
red pepper flakes

Roll the dough out into a 12-inch (30-cm) long oval and place on an oiled baking sheet. Brush the dough with oil and sprinkle with salt then build your flower garden on top.

Use a paring knife or scissors to cut "petals" out of bell peppers, removing the seeds. Cut lengthwise rounds of onion to create tulip-like flowers. Parsley and sage work well as stems and leaves. Capers can be added alongside sage stems. Dried herbs can be grass, and red pepper flakes can add a decorative kick of spice.

After assembling your garden, bake according to the dough's package, or about 15 min at 425°F (220°C).

Optional: serve alongside cheese, or with marinara or pesto as a dipping sauce.

Thomas Fogarty
Winery, Woodside

LEMON-PARMESAN SMASHED POTATOES

serves 4-6

BOIL

24 oz (680 g) small potatoes
(I use about 16 bite-size
honey golds for 4 people)

*until fork-tender,
about 10 min*

NEXT

put cooked potatoes in a bowl with:
3 T olive oil
juice from ½ lemon
2 t chopped rosemary
3 T grated Parmesan
salt & pepper

& toss!

SMASH

Place the coated potatoes
evenly spaced on a baking
sheet. Use the bottom of a
glass to gently smash each
potato so that it's flatter
but still intact. Spoon any
remaining cheese mixture
from the bowl onto the
potatoes. Sprinkle salt
and pepper over all.

BROIL

5 min each side,
until golden &
crispy

Carrots with Mint-Caper Tapenade

serves 4-6

Wild mint growing behind our cabin in the Santa Cruz Mountains inspired this recipe.

① 8 carrots, sliced diagonally
olive oil
salt & pepper

→ Spread carrots out on a baking sheet, drizzle generously with olive oil, and sprinkle with salt and pepper. Roast at 425°F (220°C) for 35 min or until tender & just a bit crispy around the edges.

② ½ c (15 g) mint leaves
3 T capers
¼ c (25 g) walnuts
2 T olive oil
salt

→ Mix in a small food processor or use a hand blender in a jar to blend into a thick pesto-like sauce. Add a tiny bit of water if it seems too thick to blend, but some chunks are OK. Spread the sauce (tapenade) on a platter with more around the edges and a thinner area in the middle to place the cooked carrots.

③ 2 scallions, chopped
2 T pinenuts

Garnish.
Serve warm or
at room temp.

Old Bay Brussels

(just 3 ingredients!)

serves 4-6

In October when driving Hwy 1 near Half Moon Bay, we saw
fields of brussels sprouts being harvested (see page 144). They
are one of my favorite cold-weather vegetables, and I love
how quick and delicious this recipe is. Old Bay is a seasoning mix available at most grocery stores that is salty with
just the right amount of spice. If you can't find it, simply
salt and pepper with a pinch of cayenne is also delicious.

{ 6 c (540 g) brussels sprouts, trimmed & halved
  olive oil
  Old Bay seasoning

Put halved brussels on a baking sheet, drizzle generously
with olive oil, and sprinkle all over with Old Bay seasoning.
Bake at 425°F (220°C) for 20-25 min or until the edges start to
get browned and crispy. Enjoy immediately.

Half Moon Bay

Brussels, Apples & Pecans

serves 4-6

We spent a snowy weekend in Tahoe for Thanks-giving and made this very simple dish for the big meal. This veggie side is easy to make in a vacation rental with a basic kitchen.

you'll need:

3 shallots, sliced
2 T butter
olive oil
2 cloves garlic, minced
30 brussels sprouts, trimmed & halved
2 red apples, cubed (peel on)
1 c (100 g) pecans, coarsely chopped
⅔ c (95 g) dried cranberries
salt & pepper

① **Sauté** the shallots, butter, garlic, and a bit of olive oil until the shallots are translucent, 3-5 min.

② **Add** the brussels sprouts and cook 8-10 min, stirring often, until slightly browned. Add more olive oil if needed.

③ **Stir** in the apple cubes, pecans, and cranberries just long enough to warm them. Season with salt & pepper to taste and serve warm.

Delicata Squash
with tahini
serves 4-6

Growing up in Sonoma County, my parents always
had a huge vegetable garden (still do!). They grow
several varieties of squash, and this is one of
my favorites. It's especially pretty when cut
into rounds. If you can't find it, try using
slices of acorn squash or peeled butternut.

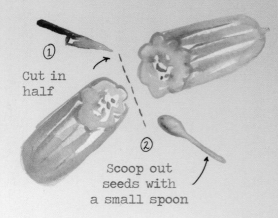

① Cut in half

② Scoop out seeds with a small spoon

1 large delicata squash
olive oil
salt & pepper
3 T pomegranate seeds
1 scallion, chopped
2 T salted & roasted pistachios, chopped
2 T tahini
1 lemon wedge

Cut the squash in half widthwise, then use a small spoon to remove the
seeds. Cut the squash into approx. ½-inch rings (discarding ends). Put the
rings on an oiled baking sheet and sprinkle with olive oil, salt & pepper.

Bake at 400°F (205°C) for about 30 min, flipping halfway through to brown both
sides. When fork-tender, remove squash and transfer to a platter.

Top with a sprinkling of pomegranate seeds, scallions & pistachios. Drizzle
the platter with tahini, olive oil, and a squeeze of lemon. Sprinkle the
platter with flaky salt & pepper and serve warm or at room temp.

The Sonoma Coast

green Soup

serves 4-6

Soup actually travels quite well in jars in a cooler when driving to a rental house. Just heat and serve when you arrive! Even better, keep it hot in a thermos and it's a healthy roadside meal. This soup is adapted from my mother-in-law Wendy's recipe. It's a light soup but still creamy and I love that it includes lettuce! It's originally inspired by cookbook author Lee Bailey's recipe, but Wendy has adapted it over the years, and here I've made it vegetarian by using vegetable stock. It's almost dairy-free except for the butter, which adds a nice richness, but you can use olive oil in its place and skip the sour cream topping to make it vegan.

SAUTÉ 10 MIN in a large pot

- 3 medium onions, chopped
- 3 cloves garlic, sliced
- 3 T butter
- salt & pepper

THEN ADD:

4 c (960 ml) vegetable broth
2 russet potatoes, cubed (no need to peel)

bring to a boil then simmer 10 min or until potatoes are fork-tender

NEXT ADD
3 handfuls greens

Feel free to use up whatever greens you have on hand. I like a mix of spinach, arugula, and lettuce. Turn off the heat and stir to wilt, then blend in the pot using an immersion blender. Add more broth if needed to reach desired consistency.

GARNISH

with chopped scallions, yogurt or sour cream, a few greens pan-fried in butter or olive oil, salt & pepper

Palm Desert

Cashew - Cauliflower Soup

serves 4-6

This soup is perfect after a day of skiing. It can also be made ahead and stored in jars to bring in an ice chest on a road trip.

① 3 medium onions, diced
3 cloves garlic, minced
pinch of salt
½ t fresh thyme
3 T butter
} **sauté in a big pot 5-7 min**

② **then add** →
1 medium head cauliflower, chopped
2 c (480 ml) veg broth
2 c (480 ml) cashew milk (or almond milk)
¾ c (90 g) roasted & salted cashews
juice from ¼ lemon
salt & pepper

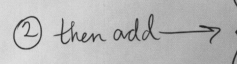

③ **Simmer on med/low 10 min or until cauliflower is fork-tender**

④ **Blend!** I use a hand blender right in the pot. Add more vegetable broth if needed to achieve desired consistency.

⑤ **garnish** with chopped roasted & salted <u>cashews</u>, chopped <u>scallions</u> & <u>olive oil</u>

Stanislaus National Forest

the Eastern Sierras

De La Cour Ranch,
Lone Pine

Driving up Hwy 395, we stopped at De La Cour Ranch, an innovative eco-farm nestled in a valley in the Eastern Sierras. We rented one of their cabins for a couple nights and loved it. This area was formerly inhabited by the Paiute for thousands of years, and with its dramatic views, it truly has a mystical, magical feeling to it. Julie, who runs the ranch, welcomed us and gave us a tour of her U-pick lavender fields and impressive permaculture farming techniques. The boys got to pet the horses, feed the baby goats, pick plums, and gather eggs for breakfast.

De La Cour Ranch,
Lone Pine

Collecting eggs with Julie

Friends tipped us off to some
natural hot springs off Hwy 395
near Mammoth Lakes.

Here & bottom row: Bodie State Historic Park (see more info on page 66)

Left: Ezra among the rock formations of the Alabama Hills, where we stopped for a hike

BREAKFAST

The Alabama Hills

Breakfast Burritos
with APRICOT SALSA   serves 4

One of my favorite things in the world is to wake up at my aunt and uncle's beach house (page 48), take a morning swim followed by a hot outdoor shower, then eat breakfast burritos on the deck. During a summer visit, we made these one morning using apricots we'd picked the day before at Rancho San Julian (page 52). I fry the potatoes first while I make the salsa and prep the other ingredients, then use the same pan for the eggs to cut down on dishes.

for the burritos

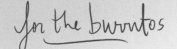

1 large potato, cut in small cubes
4 flour tortillas, warmed (I use whole wheat)
1 (15 oz/430 g) can black beans, drained & heated
6 eggs, scrambled
1-2 avocados, sliced or mashed

Sauté the potatoes in <u>olive oil</u> with a pinch of <u>salt</u> until tender and browned (about 10 min, stirring often). Place a warm tortilla on each plate and spoon/sprinkle the other ingredients on top. Add the salsa below as a final topping. Wrap and enjoy!

for the salsa

mix in a bowl & serve on the side as a topping

3 apricots, diced
3 T finely diced red onion
1 tomato, diced
⅓ c (10 g) cilantro, chopped
juice from ½ lime
pinch of salt

On the beach below my aunt & uncle's house near Santa Barbara

Pink Pancakes

serves 4-6

On our longest road trip we took a box of just-add-water pancake mix, which made quick breakfasts in a new place feel special. At home, I love putting the mix in a blender and adding some raw beet to make it a fun color, plus it slightly increases my kids' veggie intake for the day without them noticing.

① mix in a blender until smooth {

store-bought <u>pancake mix</u> prepared according to package instructions (enough to make 10-12 pancakes)

<u>small beet</u>, cut in chunks

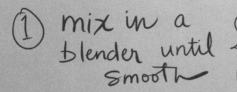

② Pour the pancake batter into 4-in (10-cm) rounds on a buttered skillet over medium heat. Flip to cook both sides. Serve hot with <u>butter</u> and <u>maple syrup</u> or agave on top.

Palm Springs

Butternut & Kale Strata

serves 4-6

California's winter is mild where we live, but we still get plenty of butternut and kale in our local farm box during the colder months. This is a hearty make-ahead alternative to quiche for brunch. It serves about 4, but you can easily double it in a 9 x 13-in (23 x 33-cm) pan for more guests (but it may need to cook a bit longer to ensure the egg is set).

sauté {
- 1 onion, diced
- 2 c (230 g) cubed butternut squash, peeled & cut into ½-in (12-mm) cubes
- 2 T butter
- 1 t fresh thyme leaves, chopped
- salt & pepper

mix {
- 6 eggs
- 1½ c (360 ml) milk
- 1½ c (170 g) grated cheese (I used smoked Gouda)
- 3 c (270 g) sourdough or rustic bread torn in 1-in (2.5-cm) pieces
- 2 c (130 g) chopped kale

Sauté the onion and squash in butter with the thyme and a bit of salt and pepper until the squash is firm but fork-tender, 10-12 min. Mix in a bowl with all the other ingredients until the bread is well coated, then pour into a greased 8 x 8-in (20 x 20-cm) baking dish. Bake at 375°F (190°C) for 40-45 min or until the egg is set and the edges are slightly browned.

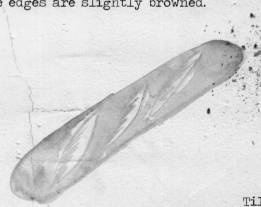

Tile wall near Palm Springs

Brussels Hash

- 2 potatoes, diced
  (I use Yukon Gold—
  no need to peel)
- 1 onion, diced
- 2 T olive oil
- 2 cloves garlic, minced

- 20 brussels sprouts, stems
  removed, thinly sliced
  into "coins"
- salt & pepper
- 4 eggs
- red pepper flakes/hot sauce

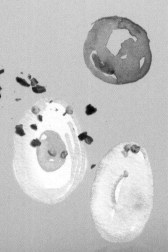

1. In a large skillet, sauté the potatoes and onion with olive oil for about 10 min or until fork-tender. Then add the garlic, brussels sprouts, salt & pepper and stir 3 min, just until the sprouts are bright green.

2. Divide the potato mixture onto 4 plates and top each with an egg cooked as desired. Garnish with red pepper flakes or hot sauce. This can also be served family-style in a casserole dish or big skillet with all the eggs on top.

Brussels sprouts
growing in the fall
in Half Moon Bay

Beet Green Egg Muffins

makes 6

This is a great way to use the greens on top of beets rather than composting them. These frittata-like muffins are perfect for a breakfast on the go!

6 eggs
½ c (85 g) crumbled feta
5 beet green leaves, finely chopped (approx. ⅓ c/10 g)
3 scallions, chopped
salt & pepper
1 small beet

Mix all ingredients (except the beet) in a bowl, then pour the mixture into 6 greased muffin tins, dividing evenly. Cut the raw beet into matchstick-size pieces and put a few on top of each "muffin."

Bake at 375°F (190°C) for 20 min or until the egg is set. Enjoy warm.

Topping options: more <u>feta</u>, <u>chopped cilantro</u>, <u>sprouts</u>, <u>salsa</u>, and/or <u>hot sauce</u>

The Eastern Sierras
off Hwy 395

SKILLET green Chile Polenta & EGGS

serves 4-6

We had some incredible Mexican food while visiting
San Diego—no wonder, given how close it is to Mexico.
We stayed in Little Italy, which had an amazing farmers'
market right on our doorstep. Inspired by Mexican and
Italian flavors, I came home and made this for breakfast.

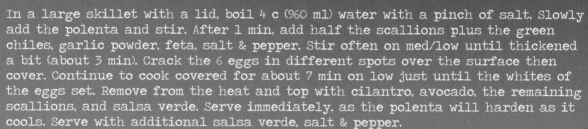

1 c (360 g) dry polenta
4 chopped scallions
3 T canned diced green chiles
½ t garlic powder
½ c (75g) crumbled feta
salt & pepper
6 eggs
3 T chopped cilantro
1 avocado, sliced
½ c (120 ml) salsa verde

In a large skillet with a lid, boil 4 c (960 ml) water with a pinch of salt. Slowly
add the polenta and stir. After 1 min, add half the scallions plus the green
chiles, garlic powder, feta, salt & pepper. Stir often on med/low until thickened
a bit (about 3 min). Crack the 6 eggs in different spots over the surface then
cover. Continue to cook covered for about 7 min on low just until the whites of
the eggs set. Remove from the heat and top with cilantro, avocado, the remaining
scallions, and salsa verde. Serve immediately, as the polenta will harden as it
cools. Serve with additional salsa verde, salt & pepper.

Farmers'
market in
Little Italy,
San Diego

Challah Cinnamon Rolls

makes 8 rolls

I was nine months pregnant when the pandemic started, and I began baking bread at home like everyone else, mostly challah for Shabbat. My Grandma Winnie, who lived near us in Sonoma County growing up, always made cinnamon rolls on weekend mornings. I found myself making a double batch of challah dough on Fridays so I could do the same. When the baby arrived, we named her Winnie, and this cozy recipe reminds me of that sweet time at home in the cabin with our new family of 5. These are lightly sweet morning rolls (not the sticky, gooey variety) and are lovely with a cup of coffee.

note: I prep the rolls in the evening and bake the next morning.

① 1 packet instant yeast (1 T)
1 c (240 ml) warm water
⅓ c (75 g) brown sugar
1 egg
1 t salt
⅓ c (80 ml) vegetable oil

} *mix in a standing mixer with a dough hook*

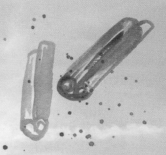

② Next add 3-4 c (375-500g) all-purpose <u>flour</u>, little by little, until a dough forms that doesn't stick to the bowl. It should feel like playdough and not be too sticky. I prefer a mixer, but if you do it by hand, be sure to knead for about 5 min.

③ Cut the dough into 8 pieces and, using your hands, roll each into a rope (approx. 8 in/20 cm long). Slightly flatten the ropes with your fingers on a large cutting board. Spread room-temperature <u>butter</u> on each and sprinkle generously with <u>brown sugar and cinnamon.</u> Roll each into a coil, pinch closed, and place in an oiled 8 x 8-in (20 x 20-cm) baking dish. Cover and refrigerate overnight. In the morning, let them sit in a warm spot for 30-60 minutes before baking.

④ *Bake at 350°F (175°C) for about 35 min or until golden*

When they come out of the oven, drizzle the buns with <u>honey</u> and sprinkle with <u>kosher or flaky sea salt.</u> Serve warm with <u>butter.</u>

Zucchini Breakfast Sandwiches

serves 4

After visiting Rancho San Julian (here & page 52) we took home more zucchini than we knew what to do with, which inspired this breakfast. I love sneaking grated squash into my kids' eggs, and they rarely notice, especially if it's in a sandwich.

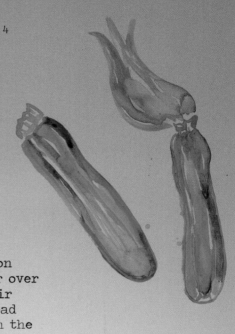

1 medium zucchini, grated (about ½ c/55 g)
1 T butter
3 eggs
1½ c (170 g) grated smoked Gouda cheese
1 T chives
salt & pepper
3 T mayonnaise
4 whole-wheat English muffins, halved & toasted
1 handful arugula
Sriracha, to taste

Sauté the grated zucchini with butter for 2 min on med-low, then add the eggs and grated cheese. Stir over medium until scrambled. Turn the heat off and stir in the chives, plus a pinch of salt & pepper. Spread mayonnaise on each English muffin, then top with the egg mixture. Add a bit of fresh arugula, salt & pepper to each sandwich. Add sriracha as desired.

Rancho San Julian
near Santa Barbara

Peach Breakfast Pops

serves 4-6

We had fun picking peaches in Brentwood. After we'd eaten and baked with as many as we could, we froze some for smoothies and made some into popsicles. These are just healthy enough to have for breakfast on a hot day. Use a nondairy yogurt like cashewgurt for a vegan version.

3 peaches
½ c (75 g) blueberries
1 c (240 ml) vanilla yogurt
} mix in a blender

Pour into about 6 popsicle molds, add a sprinkle of granola on the bottom of each (you'll need a few tablespoons), then add the stick. Freeze until solid and enjoy!

Picking peaches in Brentwood

Humboldt

The Ranch House at the Humboldt
Bay Social Club in Samoa

We made the Humboldt Bay Social Club in Samoa our home base for a few days and really loved it. They have several houses and cabins you can rent that have been thoughtfully designed by the owners, Jon and Amy. This kitchen was a dream to cook in!

In the evenings we walked over to the Lobby Bar for s'mores and cocktails around the fire pit. Beyond the bar is the Samoa Drag Strip, where we had fun watching locals race cars.

Top row: The Ranch House at the Humboldt Bay Social Club

Here: Behind the Ranch house there's a path through the eucalyptus grove to Oyster Beach. The town of Eureka is across the water.

Here & bottom right: Arcata farmers' market

Top right: Shrine's Drive-Thru Tree, visitredwoods.com

Below: Avenue of the Giants

In Prairie Creek Redwoods State Park near Humboldt, we stopped at Fern Canyon Trail, which is an incredible walk along a riverbed flanked by towering fern-covered walls.

MAINS

Trinidad

Walnut Enchiladas

serves 4-6

When I was little we had a walnut tree in the front yard, and we passed miles of them driving through the Central Valley. I love the protein and crunch they add here.

for the filling

1 c (80 g) mushrooms, chopped
1 red onion, diced
¾ c (90 g) unsalted walnuts, chopped
1 (15 oz/430 g) can black beans, drained

sauté the mushrooms & onion on med-low with <u>olive oil</u> & a pinch of <u>salt</u> for 8-10 min.

then stir in the walnuts & beans until warm.

Next you'll need
- 8 corn tortillas or small flour tortillas, heated in a pan or over an open burner flame
- 1 (16 oz/480 ml) jar red enchilada sauce
- 1 approx. 7 x 12-in (17 x 30-cm) casserole dish

Start rolling!

Pour ½ c (120 ml) sauce into the bottom of the dish, then start rolling a few spoonfuls of filling into each tortilla and place them seam side down in a row. Fit as many tortillas as you can, then sprinkle any leftover filling on top. Pour the remaining sauce over the tortillas and sprinkle with 1 c (115 g) grated <u>cheddar cheese</u>.

Bake at 375°F (190°C) for 20-25 min

serve with <u>sour cream</u> & <u>avocado</u> on the side

Creamy Cashew Pasta

serves 4-6

Vegan creamy pasta sauce made from soaked cashews has become popular in recent years, and this is my simplified take on it. It's reminiscent of alfredo, but nondairy and a bit more garlicky. It's best just out of the blender on hot pasta, so be sure to eat it right away. Get creative by topping the pasta with your favorite cooked vegetables.

2 c (240 g) roasted salted cashews, soaked in water 1 hr
juice from 1 lemon
1 1/4 c (300 ml) hot veg broth
2 cloves garlic
salt & pepper

Strain the cashews then blend with all other ingredients on high until very smooth. Feel free to add a bit more broth to reach desired consistency. Stir the sauce into 12 oz (340 g) strained, just-cooked, hot pasta. Sprinkle with chopped scallions, olive oil, salt & pepper and enjoy immediately.

Driving toward
Mt. Lassen in Lassen
Volcanic National Park

Sweet Potato Chili  serves 4-6

This dish is gluten-free and can be vegan if you use non-dairy sour cream. It's easily made ahead, good for a group, and the toppings make it fun to serve bar-style.

in a big pot...

(1) 1 red onion, diced
1 red bell pepper, diced
3 cloves garlic, minced } sauté on low 5 min
2 T olive oil
salt & pepper

(2) then add {
1 t cumin
2 t chili powder
2 t Bragg Liquid Aminos (or soy sauce)
1 (28 oz/794 g) can diced tomatoes
2 c (480 ml) veg broth
1 (15 oz/430 g) can black beans, drained
3 c (405 g) cubed sweet potato, peel on (2-3 sweet potatoes)

(3) Stir and simmer on low about 45 min-1 hr, or until sweet potatoes are fork-tender and much of the liquid has reduced.

Optional (if you like it spicy): At the end you can add 6 oz (170 g) <u>soy chorizo</u> for added flavor, texture, and spice, and/or a couple pinches of <u>cayenne pepper</u>.

topping ideas {
avocado
diced onion
sour cream or
   Greek yogurt
scallions
cilantro
hot sauce
sliced radishes
tortilla chips

Campovida winery, Hopland

Skillet Tofu & Onions

serves 2-4

This is the first book I've included tofu in! But my hippie Sonoma County upbringing was full of it, so I figured it was time. This is one of my favorite ways to eat tofu, and Jon and I make this often for weeknight dinners. It can be put on top of rice, noodles, or salad and serves 2-4, depending on what you're serving it with. One block of tofu fits easily in our large skillet with none overlapping, so if you double the recipe you may need to make it in batches. Hint: load and cover the skillet before turning it on, as the oil tends to spit.

① in a large skillet fry on medium (covered) until golden, about 10 min

{
2 T olive oil
1 T sesame oil
14-oz (397-g) block of firm tofu, cut into about 16 squares
½ t garlic powder, sprinkled on top of tofu in pan
}

② flip the tofu

③ {
1 medium red onion, thinly sliced in circles
1 T everything bagel seasoning
2 T Bragg Liquid Aminos (or soy sauce)
}

add to the skillet & cook 5-7 more min stirring once

Hwy 1 near Big Sur

Spaghetti Squash Taquitos

makes 12

Taquitos have become one of our go-to weeknight dinners at home. They come together quickly and it's one of the only ways the boys will eat beans! When spaghetti squash comes in our farm box in the winter, this is one of my preferred ways to use it, but you can add almost any kind of chopped or mashed cooked vegetables to the filling. Potato, sweet potato, and butternut squash are some other favorites.

you'll need:

- 1 medium spaghetti squash
- olive oil
- salt & pepper
- taco seasoning
- 12 corn tortillas
- 1 (15 oz/430 g) can refried beans
- 1 c (115 g) grated cheese
- guacamole, salsa, and/or sour cream for serving

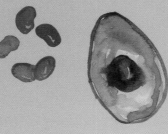

① Bake the Squash

Cut the squash in half lengthwise, spoon out the seeds, and bake face-up, drizzled with olive oil, salt, and pepper at 400°F (205°C) for about 45 min. You'll know it's done when you can scrape a fork and it pulls up the squash strings easily. When it's done, scoop all the squash into a bowl and mix with taco seasoning to taste (about 1 t seasoning per 1 c squash).

② Fill the tortillas

Warm each tortilla over an open flame or in a pan to ensure they don't crack when rolled. I do 4 tortillas at a time. Put a spoonful of beans, cheese, and squash in each tortilla and roll.

③ Fry!

Heat a thin layer of olive oil in a large skillet and place the taquitos seam side down. Cover and fry until golden and crispy, flipping once.

serve with guacamole, salsa, and/or sour cream for dipping

Hwy 1 near Point Reyes Station

Acorn Squash Bowls

serves 4

We loved visiting the farm at Fairview Gardens in Goleta (here & page 51). They are a nonprofit dedicated to sustainability and education surrounding healthy food and farming, and I learned so much.

2 medium acorn squash

> ① Cut in half lengthwise, remove seeds, drizzle with <u>olive oil</u> and sprinkle with <u>salt</u>, then bake at 400°F (205°C) face-up for 35 min or until fork-tender.

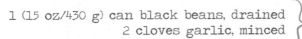

1 (15 oz/430 g) can black beans, drained
2 cloves garlic, minced
> ② sauté until warm

2 ripe avocados, cubed
1 handful cilantro, chopped
½ c (120 ml) sour cream
4 radishes, trimmed & sliced into rounds
> ③ Toppings

④ Spoon the bean mixture into each squash bowl then add toppings

Fairview Gardens, Goleta

Tortilla Pie

serves 4-6

Inspired by the abundant flavors of Mexico found all over California, this is an adaptable recipe that comes together quickly. I used spinach, but feel free to be creative and add any sautéed vegetables you'd like to the layers. Be sure to look for soft taco-size tortillas that will fit inside a pie dish.

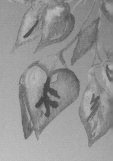

PREHEAT OVEN to 400°F (205°C)

1 onion, diced
1½ c (160g) raw cauliflower "rice"
olive oil
salt
1 (15oz/430g) can black beans, drained

1 handful spinach, chopped
10 oz (300ml) red enchilada sauce
4 whole wheat tortillas (look for soft taco size, approx. 8-in/20-cm diameter)
¾ c (85g) grated cheddar cheese

Sauté the onion and cauliflower with olive oil and salt for 8-10 min. Then add the beans, spinach, and 8 oz (240 ml) of the enchilada sauce and stir until warm, about 3 min.

Lay a tortilla into the bottom of a 9-in (22 cm) round pie dish. Next spread ⅓ of the bean mixture, then cover with another tortilla. Repeat to create 2 more layers. Finish with a tortilla on top of the stack. Pour the remaining 2 oz (60 ml) sauce over the top tortilla and sprinkle the cheese on top.

BAKE at 400°F (205°C) for 15 min

Garnish with sour cream, salsa, green onions, and cilantro. Cut into wedges and serve warm.

Next time I visit Capitola, I'd like to stay in one of these houses along the river that leads to the beach.

Chickpea Stew

On a road trip down Hwy 1, the coastal town of Half Moon Bay
is a fun stop. It's not far from where we live, and every October
we visit Bob's Pumpkin Farm with our friends Margaret and
Austin and their kids Whitney and Calder. In this area it's
common to see clam chowder served in a bread bowl, which
inspired this dish. I had something similar for dinner once
at the Half Moon Bay Brewing Company, our go-to spot for
outdoor happy hour with an ocean view.

in a pot...

sauté 5 min {
1 onion, diced
2 cloves garlic, minced
2 T olive oil

↓

then add these {
3 carrots, cut into small cubes
1 Yukon Gold potato, cut into small cubes
1 (15 oz/430 g) can chickpeas, drained
2 c (480 ml) vegetable broth
juice from ½ lemon
½ t curry powder
salt & pepper

Simmer and stir until the potatoes are fork-tender. Spoon the hot stew into
hollowed-out sourdough bread bowls that are a bit bigger than dinner rolls.
Kaiser rolls can also work. Garnish with chopped scallions and add salt &
pepper to taste. Depending on the bread bowls you find, it should be enough
filling for about 6. If there's any leftover stew, bring it to the table in case
guests want to refill their bowls or have more to dip their bread in.

Eggplant Salad SANDWICHES

makes 4

After a trip to the Saturday farmers' market in downtown Santa Barbara, we stopped for lunch at Natural Cafe on State Street, where I got a grilled eggplant sandwich that inspired this one. My version riffs on egg salad and adds cucumber for crunch. It's also great open-faced on sliced bread or serve scoops of it on salad.

① sauté
{
1 large eggplant, cut into small cubes (peel on)
1 small red onion, diced
2 cloves garlic, minced
¼ c (60 ml) olive oil
salt & pepper
}

Once the eggplant and onion mixture becomes translucent (about 8 min, stirring often), cool it and mix in a bowl with:

② mix
2 T grainy mustard
2 T mayonnaise
⅓ c (20 g) chopped scallions
2 T chopped fresh dill

③ spread
Spread the eggplant mixture onto 4 ciabatta rolls, adding thinly sliced cucumber to each.

Santa Barbara

Raw Zucchini Sandwiches

serves 2-4

With a nod to the incredible Vietnamese and Korean food around the Bay Area, I like to make these baguette sandwiches in the summer when we have an abundance of squash. They are bánh mì inspired, with the addition of kimchi and thin zucchini strips. They are great for a warm summer night's dinner, and they also pack well for a picnic. One baguette makes 2 large sandwiches or 3-4 smaller ones. Look for a vegan jar of kimchi without fish in it.

YOU'LL NEED

- 1 baguette, preferably seeded
- 1-2 zucchini, cut into long, thin strips using a mandoline or peeler
- 1 large carrot, grated
- a few spoonfuls kimchi
- ⅓ c (10 g) cilantro leaves
- ½ lime
- salt

for the spread

mix
- ¼ c (60 ml) mayonnaise
- 2 cloves garlic, grated
- 1 t sriracha (or more)
- squeeze of lime

Halve the baguette lengthwise. Smear the spread on both sides of the bread then lay down strips of zucchini. Layer each of the other ingredients then add a squeeze of lime and a sprinkle of salt. Cut into 2-4 sandwiches.

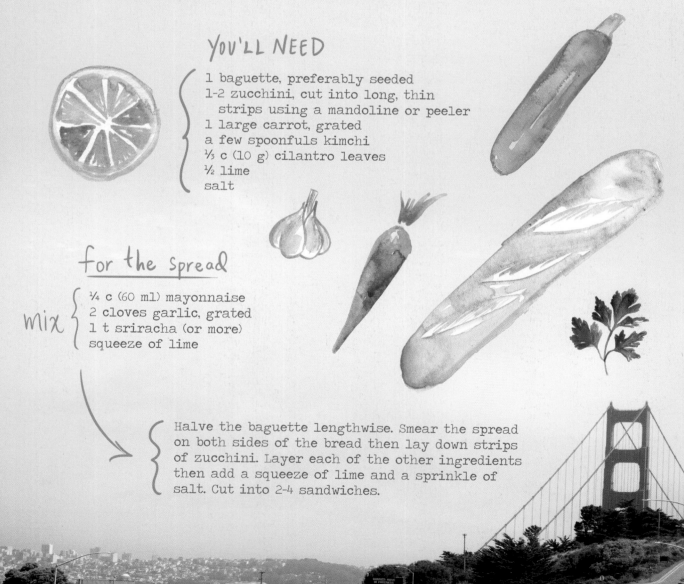

The Golden Gate Bridge, San Francisco

Veggie Spaghetti

serves 4-6

Spaghetti is always a simple, quick meal, but it's an especially good choice in a kitchen you don't know after a long day on the road. We found that these ingredients travel well and we could serve the dish bar-style to please everyone's preferences. At home, it's a go-to for weeknights. Plan for about 2 oz (55 g) dry pasta per person, and feel free to swap in your favorite vegetables. Spiralized zucchini "noodles" are increasingly common in grocery stores, but you can also spiralize yourself, use a peeler to make ribbons, or simply chop the zucchini.

- 8 oz (225 g) whole wheat spaghetti
- 4 oz (115 g) zucchini "noodles"
- 1 (24 oz/720 ml) jar marinara sauce, heated
- 12 oz (340 g) meatless meatballs (we like the Gardein brand), sautéed in olive oil
- ½ c (30 g) grated Parmesan
- ⅓ c (10 g) fresh basil, chopped
- red pepper flakes
- salt & pepper

(1) Boil the pasta, throwing the zucchini in to blanch for the last minute. Strain.

(2) Serve all other items separately so each person can build their own spaghetti bowl.

Big Sur

Halloumi Bowls

serves 4-6

To me, this is vegetarian comfort food. It's a warming bowl
of hearty vegetables topped with halloumi, a thick, salty,
satisfying cheese that can be fried without melting.

<u>8 oz (225 g) halloumi, sliced</u>

Fry in a pan with 1 T <u>olive oil</u> until
golden & crispy, about 3 min on each
side. Remove from pan, set aside, and
then add these ingredients to the pan:

SAUTÉ 15-20 min
covered, stirring
occasionally, until
squash is fork-tender
& slightly golden

4 carrots, cubed
1 large red onion, cubed
3 c (345 g) cubed butternut squash
2 T olive oil
1 t garlic powder
½ t cinnamon
½ t chili powder
salt & pepper

Add the halloumi back into the
pan for the last 2 min, just to
reheat. Serve in bowls and top
with <u>scallions and cilantro.</u>
<u>Serve over rice.</u>

We rented a cottage near the
river and walked this path to the
beach every morning in Capitola.

Pita Tostadas
—2 ways—

serves 4

Tostadas made using a crispy corn tortilla as a base are often seen in Mexican restaurants. Here I'm swapping in a soft round of pita bread to build an open-faced sandwich of sorts. I created one with Mediterranean flavors and the other with Mexican-inspired ingredients. These are also fun to serve bar-style.

Mexican

4 pitas, warmed

1 (15 oz/420 g) can refried
black beans, warmed

2 avocados, mashed

½ c (120 ml) Mexican crema
or sour cream (can be nondairy)

⅓ c (80 ml) salsa verde

⅓ c (10 g) cilantro, coarsely chopped

taco seasoning or
chili powder for garnish

Using the beans as a base,
layer the ingredients on the
4 pitas in the order above.

serve with lime wedges

Mediterranean

4 pitas, warmed

1 c (240 ml) hummus

½ c (120 ml) babaganoush

1 tomato, diced
½ cucumber, diced (peel on)
2 green onions, chopped
¼ c (40 g) crumbled feta
⅓ c (50 g) chickpeas
(from a can, drained)

} STIR

Spread hummus, then
babaganoush, onto the pita,
followed by the tomato mixture.

serve with lemon wedges

Mono Lake is salty and has these
unique rock formations called tufas.

Lentil-Edamame Bowls

makes 4 bowls

1 sweet potato, peel on
olive oil
salt & pepper
4 c (800 g) cooked lentils
2 c (310 g) shelled edamame beans
Everyday Sesame Vinaigrette, p.80
6 oz (170 g) baked marinated tofu, cubed
½ c (15 g) fresh cilantro leaves
3 scallions, chopped
1 avocado, sliced

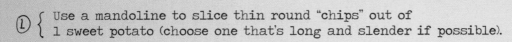

① { Use a mandoline to slice thin round "chips" out of
1 sweet potato (choose one that's long and slender if possible).

② { Spread the chips out on a baking sheet and drizzle generously
with olive oil, using your hands to coat them. Sprinkle with salt &
pepper. Bake at 425°F (220°C) for 15-20 min, just until some edges start
to brown (they should have some crunchy and some soft bits).

③ { Mix the lentils, edamame, and some of the Everyday Sesame
Vinaigrette (page 80). Divide among 4 bowls.

④ { Top each bowl with tofu (I look for a sesame, ginger, or
teriyaki flavor), cilantro, scallions, and avocado. Add a
big pile of the sweet potato chips when they come out of
the oven and a bit more salad dressing over each bowl.

Big Sur

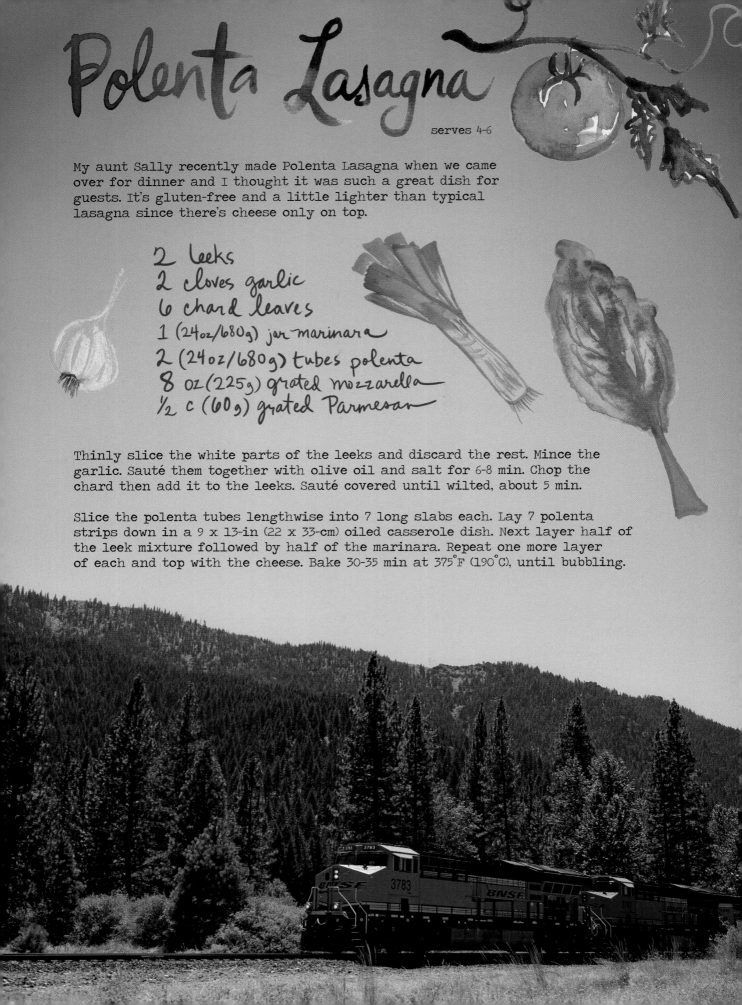

Polenta Lasagna

serves 4-6

My aunt Sally recently made Polenta Lasagna when we came over for dinner and I thought it was such a great dish for guests. It's gluten-free and a little lighter than typical lasagna since there's cheese only on top.

2 leeks
2 cloves garlic
6 chard leaves
1 (24oz/680g) jar marinara
2 (24oz/680g) tubes polenta
8 oz (225g) grated mozzarella
½ c (60g) grated Parmesan

Thinly slice the white parts of the leeks and discard the rest. Mince the garlic. Sauté them together with olive oil and salt for 6-8 min. Chop the chard then add it to the leeks. Sauté covered until wilted, about 5 min.

Slice the polenta tubes lengthwise into 7 long slabs each. Lay 7 polenta strips down in a 9 x 13-in (22 x 33-cm) oiled casserole dish. Next layer half of the leek mixture followed by half of the marinara. Repeat one more layer of each and top with the cheese. Bake 30-35 min at 375°F (190°C), until bubbling.

Rainbow Tahini Bowls

serves 4-6

Health food with a hippie vibe abounds in Humboldt County, especially in the adorable coastal town of Arcata. Their farmers' market in the town square (here) is a fun community event and definitely worth a stop. Feel free to substitute tofu for the mozzarella in this bowl to make it vegan.

- 4 c (780 g) cooked brown rice (or grain of your choice), room temperature
- 2 cooked beets (boiled or roasted whole then sliced)
- 2 carrots, grated
- ½ c (15 g) cilantro, coarsely chopped
- ¾ c (120 g) chickpeas (from a can)
- ½ c (120 ml) hummus
- 4 oz (115 g) fresh mozzarella balls

divide the ingredients among 4 bowls & top with Garlic Tahini Dressing on page 80

Sunset Stir-Fry

serves 4-6

One of the nice things about renting a beach house in California is that you almost always see the sunset over the sea. Fall sunsets seem to be the most colorful where we live, and the vibrant pinks and orange hues inspire both my painting and cooking.

1½ c (140 g) thinly sliced purple cabbage
1 carrot, julienned (cut in matchstick-size strips)
1 small red bell pepper, julienned
1 small yellow bell pepper, julienned
½ red onion, sliced
2 cloves garlic, minced
1 T olive oil
1 T sesame oil
1 T soy sauce or Bragg Liquid Aminos
1 T rice wine vinegar
pinch red pepper flakes

① sauté on med 8-10 min

② Stir in ½ c (60g) whole cashews & ½ c (75g) dried cherries for the last min

Serve as is or over rice, quinoa, or noodles.

The house we rented at The Sea Ranch (page 224)

Grilled Polenta

serves 4-6

Jon started making polenta this way, and it's become one of my favorite vegetarian items to grill. It feels like a main course, and it's delicious alongside grilled vegetables or salad. Many grocery stores now sell pre-cooked rolls of polenta, which is what we use. I also look for premade sauces and salsa (pesto and marinara are also great), or feel free to make your own.

to grill — the — polenta

- slice a 24-oz (680 g) roll of polenta into 6 wedges lengthwise
- brush each piece with olive oil
- cook on a hot BBQ grill, 3-5 min on each cut side

3 TOPPING IDEAS:

①

tzatziki
chopped cucumber

②

pico de gallo
chopped scallions

③

chimichurri
fresh cilantro

Oceano Dunes Natural Preserve

Sweet Potato BAR

This is a fun and healthy way to accommodate different dietary preferences and can be made ahead. The potatoes are gluten-free, and with the right toppings these can easily be vegan. I eat them with savory toppings but my kids like them sweet. Below are some of my favorite combinations for a weeknight or when entertaining. Choose one or make them all! Look for medium sweet potatoes and serve one per person (kids may only need a half).

place the sweet potatoes on a baking sheet
and poke them with a knife a few times before baking

{ Bake at 400°F (205°C) for about 1 hr or until a fork goes in easily }

① Sweet

Nutella
agave
chopped pecans
dried coconut chips

② Spring

asparagus, chopped & sautéed
crème fraîche or sour cream
crumbled feta
capers
lemon zest
red pepper flakes

③ BBQ

cannellini beans
diced cherry tomato
sautéed chard
sunflower seeds
BBQ sauce

④ Tofu

sautéed snow peas
cubed marinated tofu
chopped scallions
chopped peanuts
cilantro
peanut sauce

Salton Sea

Choose one of the 6 items below as your main filling in corn tortillas, then add toppings!

VEGAN TACOS

serves 4-6

(1) SHIITAKE MUSH-ROOMS, (2) BEETS, (3) SWEET POTATOES: Chop & sauté on med heat with olive oil & salt until fork-tender, 8-10 min.

(6) SPAGHETTI SQUASH: My favorite! Halve, de-seed & drizzle with oil & salt, then bake the squash cut side up on a baking sheet for about 1 hour or until a fork easily scrapes up strands of squash. Toss with olive oil & a sprinkling of taco seasoning.

① ③ ④ ⑤ ⑥ ②

(4) LENTILS: Sauté cooked lentils in a pan with olive oil & taco seasoning until warm.

(5) SOY CHORIZO: Warm in a pan.

TOPPINGS

sliced radishes

cabbage shredded & tossed with lime juice, olive oil & salt

quick-pickled red onions & carrots: slice thinly & submerge for 30 min in apple cider vinegar with a few drops agave & a few pinches salt

chopped scallions

black beans

red or green salsa

guacamole or simply mashed avocado

lime wedges

fresh cilantro

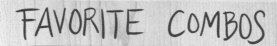

FAVORITE COMBOS

sweet potatoes,
black beans,
guacamole,
salsa

spaghetti squash,
salsa, scallions,
cabbage slaw

sautéed
beets, pickled
onions,
cilantro,
salsa

lentils,
guacamole,
pickled
carrots,
salsa

soy chorizo,
black beans,
cilantro,
radishes, salsa

sautéed mushrooms & onions,
scallions, black beans, salsa

VEGGIE Calzone Bar

serves 4-6

brush with olive oil before baking & write each person's initial in grated cheese strips

add fillings on one side then fold over & pinch to seal

poke a few holes with a toothpick before baking

I buy premade pizza dough and cut it into balls of about 6 oz (170 g) per person. It's easier to roll out when the dough is room temperature; aim for a round that's ¼ inch (6 mm) thick and about 10 inches (25 cm) in diameter. I put all the fillings in small bowls or on a cutting board and the kids love building their own. Below are four of my favorite combinations; choose one to try each week! Amounts below will fill about four calzones each.

Broccoli Rabe

{ 8-10 stalks broccoli rabe, chopped
½ onion, sliced
2 cloves garlic, minced
olive oil
salt & pepper }

Sauté 3-5 min

4 oz (115 g) fresh mozzarella
½ c (75 g) halved cherry tomatoes
¼ c (10 g) basil leaves
red pepper flakes

Scoop the cooked broccoli rabe mixture onto each dough then add other ingredients.

Chard

{ ½ onion, sliced
olive oil
salt & pepper
4 leaves rainbow chard, sliced
1 c (240 ml) ricotta
⅓ c (30 g) grated Parmesan
⅓ c (50 g) chopped kalamata olives }

Sauté the onion on med heat with olive oil & salt & pepper for 5 min, stirring in the chard at the end and covering for about 1 min, just until it wilts. Divide the ingredients among the 4 dough rounds, starting with the ricotta.

Mushroom

{ 1 c (80 g) chopped mushrooms (I use shiitake)
½ onion, sliced
2 cloves garlic, minced
½ t chopped fresh rosemary
olive oil
salt & pepper }

Sauté 8-10 min

1 c (155 g) cannellini beans (from a can, drained)
½ c (75 g) halved cherry tomatoes

Scoop the cooked mushroom mixture onto the dough rounds followed by beans and tomatoes on each.

Eggplant

{ 2 c (160 g) cubed eggplant
½ onion, sliced
½ bell pepper, diced
2 cloves garlic, minced
olive oil
salt & pepper }

Sauté all for 8-10 min, or until the eggplant is translucent and a bit browned. Spoon the mixture onto the dough rounds along with 1-2 oz (28-55 g) fresh mozzarella on each.

BAKE at 475°F (245°C)

on an oiled baking sheet for 15-20 min or until golden

Growing up, we used to leave after work on Fridays to make the four-hour drive to Tahoe to ski for the weekend. My mom always packed French rolls that had been hollowed out and filled with a bean and corn mixture. She wrapped them in foil and dish towels to keep them warm and pulled them out for dinner halfway there. These veggie-stuffed calzones remind me of those dinners on the road, and while they'd work similarly for a long evening drive, most often we make them on weeknights.

Palm Springs

We rented this amazing house in La Quinta, near Palm Springs, for a long weekend with Jon's brother Ethan, our sister-in-law Arielle, and their kids, Caleb and Zoe (here & right).

California is amazing in that the northern climate is drastically
different from the southern, allowing for a wide range of produce
to be grown year-round. One of the highlights of creating this book
for me was visiting Flying Disc Ranch, a date farm in Thermal near
Palm Springs. On a warm January morning we met farmers Robert
(here) and Christina (opposite, walking with Arielle, Jon, Robert,
and kids), who showed us their remarkable date palms which do well
grown alongside citrus. Dates grow in clusters high up in the trees
and are harvested and eaten right away—no drying or processing is
necessary. We got to try several varieties, and I had no idea that
they all tasted so different!

Here & right: blood oranges
& persimmons at the farmers'
market in La Quinta in winter

Left: Joshua Tree National Park

It was fun to go for a drink at
the Parker Palm Springs hotel.

SWEETS

Joshua Tree National Park

Date Shakes

After a visit to Flying Disc Ranch, we went home with bags of dates and made some of these shakes for an afternoon treat by the pool. Date shakes are a popular blended ice cream drink we saw all over the Palm Springs area; my version is nondairy and a little lighter. I used Medjool dates, but any variety is great.

1 c (240 ml) almond milk
1 frozen banana
5 pitted dates
5 ice cubes
pinch of cinnamon

} blend until smooth & enjoy immediately

Flying Disc Ranch in Thermal

Apple sauce

makes about 2 cups

I grew up on an apple orchard in Sebastopol, and we cooked everything you can imagine with apples. I love making applesauce on Rosh Hashanah and Hanukkah with our kids now. It certainly can be made with lemon, sugar, water, and spices, but I prefer it in its simplest form: just good, sweet, in-season apples.

8 apples, peeled & cubed

Place the apple cubes in a big pot on low heat. Cook slowly, covered, stirring often, for 30-45 min. You'll know it's done when the apples are soft and it becomes a bit golden. Use a wooden spoon or the bottom of a cup to mash the apple, leaving some chunks. Enjoy warm or chilled. It should keep in the refrigerator in a jar for several days.

Central Valley

SHORTBREAD

— 3 WAYS —

serves 4-6

It's become a tradition in each of my books to have a twist on my favorite shortbread cookie recipe, and for this one I am sharing three! The base recipe is very simple, and you can add almost anything to flavor it. I created one of these after staying at a stunning lavender farm, De La Cour Ranch, in the Eastern Sierras (here and page 132). Another is inspired by the abundance of citrus grown all over the state. And the last I developed after visiting the Brown Butter Baking Company in Cayucos. Everyone recommended we stop there when driving down the coast, and now I recommend you do, too!

BASE RECIPE

1 c (2 sticks/225 g) salted butter, cut into cubes
¾ c (150 g) sugar
2 c (250 g) all-purpose flour

for Lavender Shortbread: add 1 t dried culinary lavender, finely chopped, to the base recipe above

for Meyer Lemon Shortbread: add zest from 3 Meyer lemons & juice from 1 Meyer lemon to the base recipe above

for Brown Butter Shortbread: Melt the butter cubes over med/low heat until browned, stirring often (about 10 min, just until it smells like caramel but not burned!). Allow to cool slightly then continue with base recipe. Sprinkle with flaky salt before baking.

Pulse all ingredients in a food processor until well combined. Press the dough into an ungreased 8 x 8-in (20 x 20-cm) pan and bake at 350°F (175°C) for 30 min. Allow to cool 5 min, then cut into squares. Allow to cool completely before using a fork to transfer squares to a plate.

De La Cour Ranch,
Lone Pine

Spicy Hazelnut S'mores
makes 6

In Tahoe, we rented a house with friends (see page 230). We BBQ'd one night, and after dinner Jon and Brian made s'mores in the embers with the kids. We have found that we prefer chocolate-hazelnut spread to the usual chocolate bar, and the grown-ups enjoy the spicy kick of cayenne.

you'll need:

6 long graham crackers
6 marshmallows
⅓ c (80 ml) chocolate hazelnut spread
cayenne pepper

Break the graham crackers into squares. Smear the spread on each of the squares, add a roasted marshmallow, sprinkle lightly with cayenne pepper, and make sandwiches. Enjoy warm.

1 pack battery-operated wire twinkle lights to add a little ambience to vacation rental homes when needed.

Persimmon Smoothie Bowls

On warm fall afternoons I remember my mom picking us up from school and driving straight out to the Russian River to take a swim at Mother's Beach. We'd often get a popsicle or smoothie on the way, and it felt like summer extended. I love going back there with our kids now. Guerneville has certainly changed and is much more trendy, but the swimming holes feel exactly the same.

Smoothies alone feel very California. Put them in a bowl and decorate the top, and they are much more fun! Now each fall our farm box subscription supplies a plethora of Fuyu persimmons, and I can't get enough. When you blend them, they create a very thick texture, almost like pudding. The toppings are inspired by the figs and pomegranates we saw growing in Santa Barbara and the date farm we visited near Palm Springs.

1 frozen banana
2 ripe & soft Fuyu persimmons (peeled, seeds removed)
1 c (240 ml) almond milk
½ t cinnamon
1 t maple syrup

Blend on high in a blender, divide evenly between 2 bowls, then smooth the surface of each with a spoon. Sprinkle the tops with stripes of chopped nuts or fruit, plus a sprinkle of cinnamon. I used figs, dates, pomegranate seeds, walnuts, and golden raisins. Enjoy immediately while it is still semi-frozen.

Russian River
near Guerneville

Pineapple Swirl

serves 4-6

This frozen treat is inspired by Dole Whip, which we saw all over the Palm Springs area. Dole Whip famously originated at Disneyland and is a nondairy pineapple-flavored soft serve. Be sure to use frozen bananas to achieve the right frosty texture.

blend in a food processor until smooth

2 frozen bananas
1½ c (370 g) frozen diced pineapple
1 c (240 ml) coconut milk (or other nut milk)
pinch of salt

Scoop into small cups and enjoy right away. If you're feeling fancy, pipe it for a swirly soft-serve effect. Garnish with pieces of dried pineapple (optional).

Eastern Sierras

Sticky
DATE-ALMOND
Sundaes serves 4-6

½ c (70g) roasted salted almonds, chopped
½ c (65g) pitted dates, chopped
¼ c (10g) mint leaves, chopped
1 T honey

Stir all ingredients in a mixing bowl then spoon over 4 bowls of vanilla ice cream. I prefer nondairy ice cream made from oat or cashew milk.

We saw miles of almond trees in bloom as we drove through California's Central Valley in February.

The Sea Ranch

The Sea Ranch is an intentional community on the dramatic coastline of Sonoma County. The homes there foster a specific design philosophy and dedication to the land, making it a truly special place. We rented this house for a few days and I could have stayed indefinitely. My parents and brother Ryan (opposite), who live inland from here, came to stay with us. We loved sunset cocktail hour with an epic ocean view, the beach nearby, and family meals around the giant round table (page 226).

Here and opposite: the house
we rented at The Sea Ranch

Below left: sunset happy
hour with my mom

While in Sonoma County, we visited my parents and my brother, who live in the hills near Calistoga. The area has been devastated by wildfires the last several years, and unfortunately this photo of my brother in his garden was taken just before his property and cabin were completely burned in 2020.

Lake Tahoe

I grew up visiting Lake Tahoe often
with my family and returning now
with our own kids, I am reminded of
just how spectacular it is in every
season. I love swimming in the clear,
blue water in summer and skiing in
winter. On a road trip in August, we
rented this unique octagonal house
in Carnelian Bay (here & opposite)
with our friends Dara and Brian and
their kids, Pearl and Levi. We had
so much fun rafting, swimming, and
hiking and BBQing each evening.

Kings Beach is a fun place
to spend the day swimming
and floating on Lake Tahoe.

Here: Eagle Rock Trail is a
great hike to do with kids.

Above: cooking with Dara

I think the Tahoe City farmers' market is one of the prettiest markets in California (here & right).

We spent an after-noon rafting on the Truckee River.

Lunch at the historic Sunnyside Restaurant & Lodge in Tahoe City inspired the salad on page 106.

Favorite Stops

Here is a list of some of our favorite spots around California not to be missed, and a few places off the beaten path:

If you fly into San Francisco, be sure to visit the Sonoma and Napa wine countries. I love the towns of Calistoga and Healdsburg and the wineries of the Dry Creek Valley nearby. The Russian River near Guerneville is also a fun area, especially in the summer. Other must-see places are Point Reyes, Oakland, Tahoe, and Yosemite. Farther north, be sure to hit up Mendocino and Humboldt County and the towns of Eureka, Arcata, and Trinidad.

If you fly into Los Angeles, some must-see areas within driving distance are Santa Barbara, Palm Springs, Joshua Tree, the Eastern Sierras, and San Diego.

Another great option is to fly into San Francisco, rent a car, and drive south on Hwy 1, hitting up Pescadero, Santa Cruz, Monterey, Carmel, Big Sur, Cayucos, Pismo, San Luis Obispo, Santa Barbara, and then fly home out of Los Angeles (or vice versa!).

HIKES:

TOWNS:

WINERIES & BREWERIES:

Benziger Family Winery, Glen Ellen
Brown Estate, Napa
Campovida, Hopland (page 6)
Chateau St. Jean, Kenwood
HopMonk, Sebastopol
Russian River Brewing Company, Santa Rosa
Pacific Star Winery, Fort Bragg
Savannah-Chanelle Vineyards, Saratoga
Thomas Fogarty Winery, Woodside (page 116)

FARMS:

De La Cour Ranch, Lone Pine, for U-pick
    lavender (page 133)
Fairview Gardens, Goleta, for a farm tour
    and farm stand (page 51)
Harley Farms Goat Dairy, Pescadero,
    for baby goats in spring and their shop

BEACHES:

Capitola Beach, Capitola (page 94)
Cayucos Beach, Cayucos
Goleta Beach, Goleta
Kings Beach, Lake Tahoe (page 232)
Mother's Beach at the Russian River,
    Guerneville
Oceano Dunes Natural Preserve, near
    Pismo (page 196)
Oyster Beach, Samoa (page 158)
Pfeiffer Beach, Big Sur (page 28)
Salmon Creek, Bodega Bay

STATE & NATIONAL PARKS:

Armstrong Redwoods State Natural Reserve,
    Guerneville
Big Basin Redwoods State Park
Bodie State Historic Park, a ghost town
    (page 66)
Jack London State Historic Park, Glen Ellen
Joshua Tree National Park (page 209)
Julia Pfeiffer Burns State Park (page 27)
Lassen Volcanic National Park (page 98)
Yosemite National Park (page 70)

RESTAURANTS/BAKERIES/BARS:

The bar at the Ahwahnee hotel in Yosemite
    (page 70)
Alice's Restaurant, Woodside (page 239)
The Barlow, Sebastopol, is a trendy outdoor
    complex with several great restaurants,
    bars, and shops
Big Sur Bakery, Big Sur, for a nice meal or a
    pastry to go (page 24)
Boathouse at Hendry's Beach, Santa Barbara,
    for a meal by the beach
Downtown Local, Pescadero, for coffee and
    cute vintage gift items
Erick Schat's Bakery, Bishop, for amazing
    baked goods and their famous sandwiches
Gjelina, Venice, famous for its creative,
    vegetable-centric dishes
Grizzly Manor Cafe, Big Bear, an eclectic
    local diner perfect for breakfast (page 114)
La Super-Rica Taqueria, Santa Barbara, a
    famous little taqueria
Lobby Bar at the Humboldt Bay Social Club,
    Samoa (page 158)
Madonna Inn, San Luis Obispo, for dessert
    amid fabulously pink decor!
Momed, Los Angeles, for modern Mediterranean
    fare (page 249)
Natural Cafe, Santa Barbara, for a casual,
    healthy lunch
Nepenthe, Big Sur, for the best view ever
    (page 26)
Parker Palm Springs, for a fancy-retro drink
    (page 208)
Queenstown Public House, San Diego, for a
    meal in a unique old house (page 249)
The Ritz-Carlton, Half Moon Bay, for a drink
    on their patio overlooking the ocean
Rocky Point Restaurant, Monterey, for lunch
    with an ocean view and a lawn for kids to
    run (see page 58)
San Benito House, Half Moon Bay—they have
    fire pits and our kids love to run around
    in the backyard

Seascape Restaurant, Trinidad, for brunch
perched above the sea
Shorty's Eatery, Shasta, with the historic
Litsch Store Museum next door
Sunnyside Restaurant & Lodge, Tahoe City,
for lunch on the lake (page 234)
Taqueria De Amigos, Pescadero, which is in a
gas station but trust me!

ACTIVITIES:

Arts Alive! events in Eureka, including the
summer Eureka Street Art Festival
Barn Dance at Pie Ranch in Pescadero
Canoeing/kayaking in Morro Bay
Car races at the Samoa Drag Strip
Elephant seals in San Simeon or at Año
Nuevo State Park (page 90)
Henry Miller Library, Big Sur
Manzanar National Historic Site, the site of
a World War II Japanese internment camp,
Independence
Natural hot springs off Hwy 395 near Lone
Pine (page 135)
Paiute-Shoshone Cultural Center, Bishop
(page 249)
Picking pumpkins in October in Half Moon
Bay (page 248)
Filoli, a historic home and garden to tour
in Woodside
Renting a boat on Big Bear Lake (page 114)
River rafting on the Truckee River (page 106)
Seeing the wildflowers in Palm Desert or the
Santa Cruz Mountains in early spring
Skiing in Tahoe; we love Heavenly Mountain
Resort (page 248)
The summer dahlia garden in Golden Gate
Park, San Francisco
Swimming at June Lake (page 108)
Walking across the giant Sundial Bridge in
Redding

MARKETS:

Arcangeli Grocery in Pescadero.
Ask for the garlic artichoke bread!
Isla Vista Food Co-op, Isla Vista
La Quinta farmers' market (page 92)
Pescadero Grown! Farmers' Market in
Pescadero run by a nonprofit Community
Resource Center we love called Puente
Pie Ranch, on Hwy 1 in Pescadero
Santa Barbara farmers' market (page 51)
Tahoe City farmers' market, right on Lake
Tahoe (pages 234-235)
Village Fest in Palm Springs, a fun
night market

SHOPS:

Artelexia, San Diego (page 239)
Elk Store, Elk (page 247)
Emily Joubert, Woodside
General Store, San Francisco
Pigment, San Diego (page 248)
San Gregorio General Store, San Gregorio
Umami Mart, Oakland (page 239)

PLACES TO STAY:

De La Cour Ranch, Lone Pine (page 132)
Humboldt Bay Social Club, Samoa (page 156)
Indian Springs Resort & Spa, Calistoga
The Sea Ranch, Sonoma County (page 224)
Skyfarm Yurt, Los Angeles (page 74)

For a map of these places and links to
houses we stayed in, visit theforestfeast.com

Eastern Sierras

In Oakland we stopped to visit our friends Kayoko and Yoko at their retail shop, Umami Mart, which celebrates drinks, design and Japan. Their cocktail glasses are my favorite and I used several for the Drinks section of this book.

Here: Alice's Restaurant is our beloved neighborhood spot in the Santa Cruz Mountains. We go on Thursdays for live music in the backyard.

Below left: picking peaches in Brentwood

Below right: Artelexia, a beautiful shop with Mexican art and gifts in San Diego

Packing Tips
and other ideas to get you on the road!

After driving thousands of miles around California the last couple years, we've figured out a few things that work well for us when staying in vacation rentals.

FOOD BASKET:

I like to pack a large shallow basket (mine is about 18 in/45 cm square) that will fit near the front of the car and can hold snacks and water bottles for the drive but can also hold kitchen essentials for when we arrive at a house. Surprisingly, many kitchens don't include basics like olive oil and even salt! Here's what I put in the basket: one good knife rolled in a dish towel, a small jar of kosher salt, a small jar of flaky Maldon salt, a small pepper grinder, a small bottle of extra-virgin olive oil, ground coffee, a small cone coffee dripper with #2 filters, drinks, nuts, fresh fruit, reusable food storage bags and containers (I like Stasher brand), food storage wrap (I like reusable beeswax wrap), a small container of dish soap, a sponge (this comes in handy in a hotel room), cocktails supplies (shaker, bitters), baby wipes, and a roll of small garbage bags.

PICNIC BACKPACK or BASKET:

We received one of those pre-stocked picnic backpacks for our wedding, and it's very useful on road trips! It's got all the essentials (plates, cups, silverware, a tiny cutting board, wine opener, etc.) and comes in handy when making sandwiches out of the trunk, having a picnic dinner at the beach, or if a rental house is missing something. I swapped out the plates in ours for some cute vintage melamine ones (there are lots on Etsy), and added some floral fabric napkins, a few sporks, and some small wooden bowls. I also added a tapestry tablecloth that can double as a beach blanket.

COOLER:

We recommend one that rolls and is around 40 quarts (37 liters—not huge). It saves space, and we like shopping frequently, especially at farmers' markets. We store lunch essentials like small jars of mayonnaise and mustard, avocado, cheese, lettuce, and hummus, plus a few cold drinks. We use ice packs that we re-freeze at each new house (ice gets everything wet!).

SNACKS & MEALS:

We are always looking for snacks that won't crumble all over the back seat or create sticky fingers. I bring a few stacking cups that I can load snacks into and pass around. Some favorites are dried fruit, nuts, pretzel sticks, string cheese, apple slices, carrot sticks, Tahini Balls (page 36), and Blender Muffins (page 38). (Never popcorn. Lesson learned!)

AMBIENCE:

I always pack several votive candles (about two for each night of the trip) and two mini jars to place them in, plus a battery-operated string of wire twinkle lights to hang over an outdoor dining area (see page 216). If we'll be at a house for three or more nights, I often buy fresh flowers. If a table is unattractive, I'll cover it with my tablecloth, and we bring a small Bluetooth speaker to listen to music while we cook. These easy little additions can make me enjoy an outdated space on vacation so much more!

CLOTHING & ACCESSORIES:

When it comes to clothes, we bring one big suitcase and pack individual zipper pouches for each person's clothes inside. This keeps us organized, saves space, and is easier to carry into a house. Since I bring few clothes for myself, I like to pack scarves, earrings, and other accessories to make the same out-fits feel fun and different. We always look for accommodations with a washer and dryer, and I pack individually sealed powder laundry detergent pods. I also pack a pair of flat slippers for myself to wear around the house.

ACTIVITIES:

For the car, Ezra (who is six) can spend a long time looking at his atlas. Max (who is four) loves to draw in a spiral sketchbook or play with Silly Putty. We pack each of them a canvas tote with activities to keep by their seat. Other favorites are the Magna Doodle drawing board, coloring books, and wax Wiki Stix. We also download audiobooks (they love the Magic Treehouse series) and kids' podcasts (their favorite is Circle Round). Sometimes we listen all together, but sometimes the kids listen on their own tablets with headphones, and then Jon and I can listen to a book or podcast together. All together we play games like Would You Rather or 21 Questions, or we have a road trip-specific scavenger hunt card game the kids enjoy. We try to avoid letting them watch shows as we drive, but for really long car days, we do it!

We also bring a few things to keep us entertained once we arrive. We pack a deck of cards, travel board games (like Scrabble), and art supplies like crayons, paper, and watercolors. In case the house we stay at doesn't have great Wi-Fi, we also like to download a couple movies, shows, and playlists ahead of time.

A FUN CALIFORNIA PLAYLIST:

"California" by Joni Mitchell
"California Soul" by Marlena Shaw
"Going Back to Cali" by Notorious B.I.G.
"California Stars" by Billy Bragg and
  Wilco (lyrics by Woody Guthrie)—
  our wedding song!
"Going to California" by Led Zeppelin
"California" by Childish Gambino
"California" by Josh Ritter
"Californication" by Red Hot Chili
  Peppers
"California Love" by 2Pac feat. Dr. Dre
"California English" by Vampire Weekend
"California Sun" by The Ramones
"In California" by Neko Case
"California Girls" by The Beach Boys

I like to bring a washable warm blanket & a tapestry-style sheet that can be used as a table-cloth or picnic blanket.

Pack battery string lights & votive candles to add ambience to your home away from home.

CRAZY EIGHTS

HEARTS CARD GAME

You never know what the knife situation in a rental house will be, so I like to bring one good one to make sure cooking is enjoyable.

Look for vintage melamine plates on Etsy to add to your picnic kit.

When traveling, I like to bring along a set of watercolors and a few sheets of 5 x 7-in (12 x 18-cm) watercolor paper. We all make little paintings along the way that end up being souvenirs or postcards. Painting the view is a nice way to take a break on a hike (just use a splash from your water bottle) or a fun activity once you get back to the house.

Santa Barbara

Acknowledgments

This book, as with my previous ones, was a collaboration with Jonathan. He is the mastermind behind these road trips and all the amazing travel our family has been fortunate to do. He encourages us to go bigger and farther than I probably would with three little kids, but in the end I'm always so happy we did. His ideas and overall vision really shaped this book. His research, planning, and travel intuition make our travel days run smoothly and make our lives so much more adventurous and fun in general! Thank you, mi amor.

This is the third book I have done with my amazing editor, Laura, who gives me the freedom to expand creatively and makes my work so much better along the way. Thank you, Laura, I love working with you! Thank you to Liam for designing this book with me and for putting up with my ancient ways. Thank you for making my work so much better. I'm so grateful to Mike Richards, Denise LaCongo, Deb Wood, and the entire Abrams team for helping me create this book.

Thank you to my agent, Alison, for being THE BEST. My dream career I didn't know I even wanted started when you cold-called me many years ago and I'll always be grateful.

Thank you to my dear friend Andrea Davidson (@clay_by_dre) for lending me your pottery pieces to shoot on. Thank you to Mara for keeping me on-mission, on-purpose, and for making things so much easier for me along the way. I love collaborating with you! Thank you, Emily, for your design and research assistance in creating this book!

Thank you to the hosts whose homes are featured in this book including Uncle Rick and Aunt Janet, Ilse and Meeno, Jon and Amy, the Seversons and Angela.

I am so grateful to my team of recipe testers! In addition to my core group of testers, this time we opened it up to the Forest Feast community and I was blown away at the generosity of so many readers and newsletter subscribers that volunteer tested. It was so fun to read through everyone's comments and get feedback from kitchens all over the world. Many thanks to Andrea Bakke, Anna Trinca, Anya Glenn, Arielle Traub, Janet and Rick Stich, Barbara Hooper, Beth Martorano, Britta Loudenslager, Claire Butler, Coral Cochran-Bray, Dan Ginader, Debbie Pike, Denise Bellardo, Denise Daukas, Donna Seidel, Faith D'Erasmo, Ferrin Huras, Gina Stubenvoll, Grace Hyde, Grier Ferguson, Cady Ferguson, Heidi Filippi, Holly Brink, Jacy Zegowitz, Jean Howard, Jeff Roloff, Jennie Hoenigsberg, Jessica Grosman, Jodie Porges, Jodie Sadowsky, Karen Weaver, Kathryn Beauchaine, Kim Budenski, Laura Keller, Laura Potts-Wirht, Lauren Czaplicki, Lee Spolar, Leslie Braun, Leslie Shimomura, Liz Vaisben, Margaret Jacobs, Maureen Sheehan, Maxwell Gregory, Marlene Swanson, Mary Edwards, Marni Gerber, Natalie Galati, Nicole Thompson, Rhea Gazer, Shannon Darsow, Shubhda Fajfar, Sonya Kotov, Susie Block, Suzanne McFarlin, Suzanne Phillip, Tara Fogel, Tracy Furgason, Talia Turkewitz, Valerie Hess, Wendy Ohlson, Wendy Bloch, and Yolanda Ridge.

Clockwise from top left: Russian River, Pescadero, lunch at Satellite in Santa Barbara, Lone Pine, Eastern Sierras, a market in LA, Lake Tahoe, Santa Cruz Mountains. Center: Morro Bay

Clockwise from top left:
farmers' market corn,
almond trees in bloom,
plums in Lone Pine, Hwy 1
near Big Sur, canoeing
in Morro Bay, summer
tomatoes, Elk Store in
Elk, Thomas Fogarty
Winery in Woodside

Clockwise from top left: Oceano Dunes Natural Preserve, Humboldt, Pigment in San Diego, Max sleeping, Carlene the minivan on Hwy 1, pumpkins in Half Moon Bay, Yosemite, Los Angeles. Center: skiing at Heavenly in Tahoe

Clockwise from top left: dinner at Momed in LA, Fern Canyon Trail near Humboldt, picking snap peas in Los Altos Hills, Paiute-Shoshone Cultural Center garden, Stanislaus National Forest, picking strawberries in Pescadero, Lake Tahoe, brunch at Queenstown Public House in San Diego

index

Note: Page numbers in *italics* include photos/captions.

Editor: Laura Dozier
Managing Editor: Mike Richards
Designer: Erin Gleeson with Liam Flanagan
Production Manager: Denise LaCongo

Library of Congress Control Number: 2021946860

ISBN: 978-1-4197-4425-9
eISBN: 978-1-64700-907-4

ABRAMS The Art of Books
195 Broadway, New York, NY 10007
abramsbooks.com

The Santa
Cruz Mountains